INTENTIONAL PROFIT

INTENTIONAL PROFIT

CLARE WOOD

First published in 2022 by Dean Publishing
PO Box 119
Mt. Macedon, Victoria, 3441
Australia
deanpublishing.com

Copyright © Clare Wood

All rights reserved. No part of this publication may be reproduced, stored in a retrieval system or transmitted in any way or by any means, electronic, mechanical, photocopying, recording or otherwise, without the prior written permission of the publisher.

Cataloguing-in-Publication Data
National Library of Australia
Title: Intentional Profit
Edition: 1st edn
ISBN: 978-1-925452-62-4
Category: Money/Finance/Business

Photographer credit: Chasing Studio, www.chasingstudio.com.au

The views and opinions expressed in this book are those of the author and do not necessarily reflect the official policy or position of any other agency, publisher, organisation, employer or company. The names, personal characteristics of individuals, characteristics of organisations and details of events in this book have been changed in order to disguise the identities or protect the privacy of the author's clients, staff, colleagues or employers. Any resulting resemblance to persons or organisations is entirely coincidental and unintentional.

The author's intent is to only offer information of a general nature. Any perceived slights of people or organisations are unintentional and unintended.

This publication does not represent professional advice. The strategies outlined in this book may not be suitable for every individual, and are not guaranteed or warranted to produce any particular result. Results in this publication are atypical, and no promises are made that you will experience the same successes. It should not be relied on as the basis for any decision to take action or not take action on any matter which it covers. Before acting on any advice, you should consider the appropriateness of the advice, and obtain professional advice wherever appropriate. In the event you use any information in this publication, the author and the publisher assume no responsibility for your actions, and disclaim all liability. The author and its related entities will not be liable for any loss or damage (financial or otherwise) that may arise out of your improper use of, or reliance on, the content of this resource. You accept sole responsibility for the outcomes if you choose to adopt and/or use the ideas, concepts, ideologies, philosophies, and opinions within this book.

The author, publisher or organisations are not to be held responsible for misuse, reuse, recycled and cited and/or uncited copies of content within this book by others.

The advice contained within this book is general in nature and is not intended as financial advice. Please seek advice from your own accountant or financial advisor before making any major decisions about your business or financial investments.

To my awesome husband, Shannon.

Thank you for dreaming big with me and helping me create an extraordinary life.

I love you x

CONTENTS

PROLOGUE..IX

CHAPTER 1:
THE TRUTH ABOUT PROFIT.. 1

CHAPTER 2:
INTENTIONAL PROFIT 17

CHAPTER 3:
INTENTIONAL MINDSET... 31

CHAPTER 4:
INTENTIONAL INVESTING 49

CHAPTER 5:
INTENTIONAL PLANNING 69

CHAPTER 6:
INTENTIONAL MARKETING... 95

CHAPTER 7:
INTENTIONAL PROBLEM SOLVING 117

CHAPTER 8:
INTENTIONAL GRATITUDE, GROWTH AND EXPANSION........ 143

ACKNOWLEDGEMENTS... 161

ABOUT THE AUTHOR... 163

ENDNOTES.. 164

PROLOGUE

Profit. This very word may have instantly created resistance in your mind when you read it.

"This isn't going to be an 'accounting book' is it?"

"Money is so confusing and overwhelming."

"What exactly is profit?"

"Will I have to work a lot harder to make more money?"

These are some of the questions and thoughts that can pop up when the word 'profit' is thrown around. But this book was written to help you demystify profit. I want to show you that numbers and budgeting don't need to be overwhelming. In fact, when you get the basics down, it can be empowering... even fun!

But money isn't just about spreadsheets and finances.

Your belief systems about your money and your ability to make a ton of it in your business are so powerful, so I also want to show you how to shift your money mindset so you can create a life more incredible than you ever imagined possible.

When I decided to put pen to paper to create *Intentional Profit*, I knew I wanted to write it in a way that could be accessible and enjoyable to all types of readers. It couldn't be airy-fairy. I may believe in manifesting and expansion, but I'm also an accountant by trade. I believe in facts and figures.

So, I've written this book in such a way that you'll be able to flick through, choose which sections resonate, and pick up the clear and actionable strategies at the end of each chapter that you can put to use immediately to help you earn more profit in your business with ease.

Or you can read the book sequentially from cover to cover, make notes, get inspired, then come back and do the actions and prompts.

The choice is yours. Either way, it's my hope that you find some meaningful advice in these pages that will help move your business forward and help you achieve your dreams. I don't say that lightly; I know how important your big goals are. I've always been a huge dreamer. And right now, I'm living the life of my dreams, with a clear vision of so much more in my future.

I wanted to write this book because I know that many business owners are overwhelmed by the idea of money, even though everyone's ultimate goal is to supercharge their bank balance and create a life of freedom.

I can't wait to see my book in bookstores and for readers to come and share their stories about how they have intentionally grown their profit after implementing the *Intentional Profit* framework outlined in these chapters. I'm sure you're going to blow me away with your results – I know this because I'm continually blown away by the results that my coaching clients achieve, and they're all based on the same philosophies and strategies outlined right here.

Anything is possible when you have the right mindset and take inspired action towards your goals. I want to open up that window for you around what is possible when you start working on your money goals and managing your money with confidence.

I hope you're feeling inspired and excited about the possibilities when it comes to money and wealth. I want you to feel empowered to put your CEO pants on and start to realise that knowing your numbers and reaching towards phenomenally successful results isn't that hard when you know how.

I've written this book as the ultimate road map for you to increase your profitability and to do it without working more hours. In fact, I want you to achieve profit goals beyond your wildest dreams, while doing life in a way that works for you – and in the following pages, I'm going to show you exactly how.

I can't wait to help you build your most intentional and profitable business.

Clare Wood x
Money Mentor
BComm (Accounting), CPA

To grab the bonuses mentioned through this book,
go to **www.clarewood.com/intentionalprofit**

INTENTIONAL PROFIT

CHAPTER 1:
THE TRUTH ABOUT PROFIT
(IT'S NOT WHAT YOU THINK)

When I'm having a really busy day and I need to recharge my batteries and steal a few moments of downtime to gather my thoughts, I head out to my backyard. I take a short walk across the grassy, flat yard and hop down beyond the fence to the sand.

I take a few more steps until my feet are underwater. And I stop.

After a couple of deep breaths, I notice the fish swimming nearby and the gentle movements of the water. I can almost feel the gratitude literally washing over my body.

Look at this life. How did I manage to end up here?

It's been my dream to own a waterfront home for many years now, but I didn't believe it could happen so soon. I thought it was a 'one day' goal. But my experiences over the last half a decade or so, since I left my corporate job and started my own business, have shown me that absolutely incredible things are possible.

Now, in the interest of full disclosure, our waterfront home is far from perfect. In fact, we call it 'the beach shack'. When we bought it, it had no working kitchen, a bright pink toilet, disgusting carpets I'm pretty sure had never been cleaned, and was overgrown with weeds and trees. We've done some minor renovations to make it clean and livable, but it's very small, very tired, and it needs a total knockdown and rebuild. That's exactly what we have planned for it – our dream mansion.

But every morning when I wake up and head to the kitchen to make a cup of coffee to start my day, watching my young boys eat their breakfast while I look out my kitchen window at the water, I'm a little bit gobsmacked. Sitting in my beachfront home prompts me to acknowledge just how far I've come, and my concept of goal setting and achievement gets amplified even more in terms of what I previously thought was possible.

There's something else I want to share, too…

Even though I live in total gratitude for what I've achieved, I also 'knew' this home was in my future.

Just as I knew I'd hit a monthly income in my business equivalent to what some people earn in a year.

I knew I'd be able to help my clients amplify *their* businesses with massive results, too.

And I know I'll be running a multimillion-dollar business in years to come.

When something amazing happens in my life, such as when I hit an income goal or have a successful course or program launch, it's amazing. I celebrate. I'm beyond excited! But I live with such intention, knowing that I can bring it to life – so I'm not surprised by these results.

I live in the vibration before I live in the reality. In my house right now, for instance, I might wake up every day in a poky, cramped little home with one bathroom. But I can so clearly see our vision for a beautiful, grand six-bedroom residence with a pool on this block of land, I'm already living it. I've practically picked out towels to match the bathroom tiles in my ensuite.

Now, some of you will be nodding along right now, like, *I totally hear you, Clare. I live with intention, and this type of manifesting shows up in my life all the time!*

But if this doesn't resonate for you or you totally don't get it, that's fine too. Some people don't understand living an intentional life until they're actually living in it.

Before you get too concerned, like, *What is this woman even going on about and why did I pick up a book about profits and we're here talking about vibrations?!* I want to share a little more about me. A quick window into my world, and how I ended up here, helping business owners transform their struggling, tired or simply underperforming service-based businesses into profitable, thriving enterprises.

I'm married to the love of my life, Shannon, and we have two young sons. At the time of writing this book, we have just moved to the gorgeous Gold Coast in Queensland, Australia, and bought an old house on a perfect waterfront block of land where we plan to build the dream home I mentioned.

I was raised as one of five children. For the majority of my upbringing, Dad was a travel agent, making a basic salary. Mum ran a family day care business – babysitting other children in our own home – in between raising me, my two sisters and my two brothers.

The best way I can think to describe my upbringing is... we had no luxury. While we never went without and always had food, clothes, school bags and school shoes, we never had anything extra, either. We didn't go on holidays, never ate at restaurants. Eating out for breakfast on a weekend, stopping at a cafe for a coffee and banana bread, or getting a 'treat' when running errands with Mum – these are all things my kids experience regularly, but it just did not happen when I was growing up. The budget was *tight*.

Note, I said we lived with 'no luxury' and not that we lived in poverty. I recognise that as an able-bodied, straight, white person growing up in a lower-middle class family, who was able to access university-level education, I have far more privilege than most people on the planet. I'm not playing the 'poor me' card but simply highlighting that I certainly wasn't born into a wealthy family or a wealthy mindset.

Eventually, my dad decided he was sick of being on struggle street, so he went to university and got educated so he could get a 'solid job' and make money. He studied accounting while he was working full-time, so, for many years, we didn't see a lot of him as he was busy studying and working.

I knew it was a big sacrifice for him (and my mother) to make with a tribe of kids, but they wanted to create a better life for us. When he graduated, he got an accounting job and started making good money.

And for the first time, we didn't struggle.

I was a teenager when that shift happened. One thing that sticks with me – we used home brand toothpaste because we simply couldn't afford Colgate. And trust me, home brand toothpaste is gross. When Dad's income increased, we still mostly shopped the home brand aisles – but my parents started buying investment properties, too.

Now I look back and I can see that even after our family's income situation changed, we continued living in 'lack'. We could afford Colgate, but Mum and Dad were so used to budgeting and scrimping and making things work with less money, they continued on the same way, even though their circumstances had changed. We were still not allowed to run our small air conditioning unit because "it costs too much!" Sticking to a budget is prudent, and I'm not at all saying you should start spending up a storm as soon as you come into some money. But as you'll learn in this book, the money stories you live by dictate your reality.

So, that was my upbringing. We were on struggle street for a very long time, until Dad studied and became an accountant, and then we didn't struggle anymore.

So, can you guess what I did?

I followed in my father's footsteps, went to university, studied, and became an accountant!

Yep, I'm a qualified, certified practicing accountant (CPA). I spent six years studying business and accounting, then I embarked on a career that saw me making good money working in finance. I was a professional and went to work wearing heels and suits, and I worked hard to earn a 'good, stable' income.

EVERYTHING I THOUGHT I KNEW WAS WRONG

The story I'd learnt in my childhood was that going to uni and getting a solid job is the secret to 'not struggling'. That was my goal – to 'not struggle'. So, I made my life decisions around what I had perceived to be a truth.

Now, as accountants, we're taught to watch the bottom line. Always. We have a laser-sharp focus on the profits. It's the most important thing we keep an eye on. If your business isn't profitable, then we need to make it profitable as quickly as possible. And the best way I was taught to do that was by cutting expenses.

There's a reason why people use the phrase, "My accountant told me to stop spending money on this." It's not just a handy explanation or great excuse when you want to change suppliers. It's genuinely one of the biggest tools of the trade. Spend less, make more profit. Simple. It's maths, right? I'm willing to bet that if you've worked with an accountant in the past, they've told you to keep your expenses low. I know what we're taught to tell you, and now I know it's all wrong!

As an accountant, I was very, very good at finding ways for people to stop spending money. If profits were low or budgets were tight, I would advise an organisation to really think long and hard about any non-essential or core spending. "Do you really need to spend money on marketing? Is it delivering a clear and measurable ROI?"

I remember one company I worked for was strategising for a massive growth period. They were throwing money at marketing like nobody's business. They were hiring social media managers, strategists, branding experts – you name it. My conservative accountant brain was screaming, *Stop wasting money! How do we know this will work?*

These days, I would advise them that investing in marketing in a strategic way is a great way to open up opportunities for growth. The investments this company made *did* work, and they went through a big income leap, but, at the time, all my accounting brain could see were the outgoings and not the potential that investing had for opening up future growth.

This whole book is about money and mindset. By now, you're hopefully starting to see the journey that I've personally been on. It has been an unexpected but powerful shift, and the way my mindset has evolved has unlocked opportunities and outcomes I didn't think were possible for someone like me.

→ **Traditional accounting:**

Everything is all about profit. Make sure your business is profitable – the best way to get there is to cut expenses.

→ **My take?**

Intentional profit means getting clear on the best way to grow your long-term profit and how you will do it – even if it means you aren't necessarily making a profit straight away.

But I never used to think like this. Concepts like manifesting, abundance and living in a high vibration?! I was a trained accountant. I was all about facts and figures. I was all for living in reality, not some vibrational, intentional, airy-fairy nonsense.

Well, let's see how that 'study hard, get a good job, work long hours and earn good money' mindset worked out for me in practice.

For a while, being an accountant was fine. It was great! I moved to London for a few years, and I was earning decent money – about double what most of my friends were making. I was travelling, splashing my cash and having a great old time.

Then I moved back to Australia and worked my way up the corporate ladder, where I spent about ten years working long hours. I'd arrive at my desk by 8 am, and it was rare to walk out before 6 pm. I had a decent social life outside of work, but my career didn't set my heart on fire.

Everything was good. Work was good. Money was good. I wasn't struggling, but I wasn't rolling in 'next level' wealth.

You know what I learnt? That money is great! Having a high disposable income, I got to have some fun. I loved travelling; I loved eating out; I loved being able to buy clothes and get my hair done whenever I wanted. But I had a burning desire that I wanted even more. I remember on one of my holidays being in St Tropez and thinking, *I want to holiday on a mega yacht*. I sure as hell knew it wasn't going to happen working my average accounting 9–5.

Soon, I realised that every time I met an entrepreneur, I lit up. I was so passionate about the startup space – about trying new things, about launching new things, testing what works and what doesn't.

Around this time, I was craving something more creative. I was in my 30s and staring down the barrel of another three decades or more of working. *Is this really all there is?*

I thought about going back to uni and studying marketing, as I knew I had a creative itch that needed to be scratched. Being an accountant wasn't what I wanted to do for the rest of my life.

While I was mulling over my future and continuing to trudge along in my corporate job, I met my now-husband, fell madly in love, and quite quickly got married and fell pregnant. However, while I was on maternity leave, I was made redundant.

Little did I know then that everything I had done, everything I had learnt had all led to this point, and much bigger, brighter things were in my future.

As you're probably realising, it actually wasn't that long ago that I discovered the power of the mind. When you shift into this mindset, amazing things can happen in a really short period of time.

Everything you've been taught about profit is wrong!

The whole purpose of this book – and in particular this chapter – is to flip your concept of profit on its head and help you understand that everything we've ever been taught about profit is wrong. So, what exactly do I mean by this?

First up, I want to acknowledge that I had it all wrong for a long time, too. With my accountancy background, I was always just so focused on profit that it was a 'profit at all costs' mentality. I've since realised that this is a really small, limited way to think.

If I had followed this line of thinking in my own business, I wouldn't have had anywhere near as much success as I've had. I would have been too hesitant to hire support staff, too worried about the money coming in to unlock my most creative and motivated mindset, too cautious to invest in coaches and masterminds that have been nothing short of life-changing.

What I've realised is this: if everything in your business is focused on profit, you don't leave enough room for anything else. The marketing, the new opportunities, the networking, the collaborations, the upskilling – all of this and more falls down the priority list.

If you have the intention that you'll create a wildly profitable business *one day*, you can unlock a completely different way of doing things.

To be clear, I'm not suggesting that anyone should make rash, reckless decisions based on nothing more than self-belief. I'm still an accountant at heart! Everything I do, say and preach is all based on a firm grounding of facts, figures and reality.

Unlocking future profits

Let me give you a brief example to explain what I mean about intentionally investing for long-term profit.

A few years ago, I started following a business coach, and I just loved her vibe. I felt so called to work with her, but it was a huge investment – $3k per month to be exact. By investing in this coach, I knew this would take a big chunk of my profit.

But I mapped out a plan of what could be possible if I did have an income breakthrough as a result of working with her. I discussed it with my husband and went for it. By the end of the 12 months working together, my profit had almost doubled – and this was *after* accounting for the $3k per month investment working with the coach.

If I had been focused heavily on the bottom line, it's unlikely I would have taken the leap to make such a big investment. I'm so glad I did because it ultimately delivered me big growth, which wouldn't have been possible if I'd stayed safe and small.

Now, I want you to think about some of the biggest and most successful businesses in the world. Facebook, Twitter, Uber… these businesses weren't profitable from day one. In the very beginning, they were scrappy startups. But even as they progressed and began pitching to investors and making some serious money, they still weren't massive cash cows of profit. It wasn't until 2017 that Twitter turned its first profit: in the last quarter of 2017, they made a $91m profit based on revenue of $732m.[1] The company was founded in 2006. That's 11 years of hustling, growing, pivoting, investing, convincing others to give you money and have an absolute belief that profits are coming… *just not yet.*

Can you imagine having that mindset?

Imagine thinking, *I'm so convinced that this is going to be a success, and I'm so certain that we're going to make massive profits from this one day that I'm going to trade this business year after year after year in the red. I'm going to go backwards in terms of income versus expenditure. I'm going to invest in more infrastructure and more people and more systems and more technology, and I'm going to go and convince people to loan me millions of dollars to make this happen.*

Because I'm certain this is going to happen.

That's a seriously intentional mindset. These founders must be pitching again and again and again and again. It's easy to look at it now, once it's already a massive success, and say, "Well *of course* they were confident. It's *Twitter*." But in those early days, they would have faced all of the same hurdles, setbacks and challenges as everyone else. They would have been fielding questions left, right and centre...

Why would people want Twitter when there was Facebook, where you could post messages *and* photos?

Why would people want to use a social media site where you can only post a few words at a time, barely more than a sentence?

As an investor, why should I pour my money into this very limited social media platform?

Remember, when Twitter first started, there were no images, no videos, and you only had 140 characters to play with. Yet, its founder believed in it. He invested in its growth and convinced many others to do the same.

These businesses weren't just splashing cash and hoping for growth. I can assure you, they would have been very intentional about the decision they were making. They were creating budgets, financial plans, and forecasts and revising their plans and pivoting. Every decision would have been analysed and reviewed. It was strategic, but they made a purposeful decision to operate without turning a profit for a very, very long time.

Sometimes, businesses intentionally run at a loss, and, sometimes, they intentionally don't make a profit for a period of time – maybe briefly, or maybe for a long period.

While all businesses ultimately want to make a profit overall, sometimes it makes sense NOT to. For instance, you might decide to put your profits back into the business to grow it, investing in things like:

- **More infrastructure, systems and processes:** to set yourself up for future growth and bigger profits down the track. Setting things up as if you have a million-dollar business early on creates such a strong support system for when you eventually do grow.

- **Support staff:** especially those staff who can help you streamline processes and free up your time to generate more income. Delegating low-value tasks is such a powerful way to grow your business – but more on that later!

- **Sales-generating staff:** such as those who can actually generate leads and bring more profits into the business. A staff member who costs $80k could generate $400k in sales.

- **Professional development:** courses, coaches, masterminds, training and education to help you expand your mindset, find new ways of doing things and unlock new opportunities.

This is where having an intentional profit mindset comes in. Whatever you're doing – spending, cutting costs, growing sales, hiring staff – you need to be doing it with serious and strategic intention.

And that's what this book is all about!

I'm going to take you through all the things you need to do to move into a clear and empowered intentional profit mindset so you can make intentional decisions that help you not just reach your goals, but smash them out of the park.

In my years as a mentor, I've worked with many different industries, and I don't believe in a rinse and repeat strategy, but there are certain things every business owner can do to improve their situation. So, I'll end each chapter with an agenda for a Money Meeting, which includes a set of actionable, practical tools you can use to start transforming your profit right away.

In the pages ahead, I'll be sharing some of the strategies I share with my clients every day – the same clients who have transformed their businesses, grown their profits and experienced breakthroughs that have set them up for lasting profits well into the future.

When I ask business owners about their goals, one of the biggest things they tell me is that they want to make more money and grow their wealth. Some are courageous enough to admit that they want to be really, really rich!

But when I then ask how much time they spend on their money...

How much time they spend managing their money, planning their spending, owning their budget, creating a plan to strive towards future wealth...

Most look at me blankly.

But for you... all that's about to change.

MONEY MEETINGS

To become a master of your money, you need to carve out time to work *on* your money. The best way to do this is to book in regular money meetings.

What is a Money Meeting?

- A Money Meeting is time you schedule in to sit and focus on the money in your business (or your personal finances).
- These meetings could be anything from a five-minute check-in to a two-hour deep dive, depending on the areas you wish to focus on in the meeting and the complexity of the review.

Who to involve in your Money Meetings?

- A Money Meeting can be something you do on your own or involve other people from your money team.
- I schedule regular money meetings with my accountant, my bookkeeper, myself and my husband. In fact, I have several money meetings a week!

Money Meetings are a great ritual to focus on your finances. At the end of each chapter, I'll share some prompts for you to get started on your own Money Meetings so you can really get the most out of each chapter and develop an unshakable, profit-focused money mindset that helps you reach your goals.

CHAPTER 1
Key Points

- When it comes to earning more money, mindset and intention are just as important as the practical actions you take.

- Traditional accounting focuses on profitability, and suggests that the fastest way to get there is by cutting expenses.

- Intentional profit is focusing on your long-term profit – even if it means you aren't necessarily making a profit straight away, or have a lower profit in the short term.

CHAPTER 2:
INTENTIONAL PROFIT

WHAT IS PROFIT?

The accounting definition of profit goes something like this:

> **Profit**
> [prof-it] **noun**
> a financial gain, referring to the difference between the amount earned and the amount spent in buying, operating or producing a product or service for sale.

In other words, profit relates to how much your business actually makes after all of your expenses are paid.

In your own business right now, can you tell me off the top of your head how much profit your business made in the last month, the last quarter and year to date?

Don't be embarrassed if you don't know that answer. Over the years, I have worked with many different business owners, many turning over multiple six-figures or even seven-figures a year – and before working with me, most of them had no idea what their profit was. It's quite common.

Maybe you are all up in your numbers, and you're totally across all of this detail. If so, great! Just consider this a quick refresher.

Regardless of your starting point, by the end of this chapter, you're going to be really clear on what both the actual profit and the profit potential is in your business.

WHAT ACCOUNTANTS DON'T WANT YOU TO KNOW

There is a lot of accounting terminology, and my experience is that many accountants (I can lovingly tease the profession here as an accountant myself) love to throw around these fancy terms so you go, "Errrmmmm, ahhhhh okay how much is it?" and pay them a lot of money to make all the 'confusing finance stuff' go away.

I spent six years studying accounting, and I'll be honest: sometimes *my* head is spinning in a meeting with my accountant. The thing is, I have a great foundation in financial literacy, and I'm also not afraid to ask questions to make sure I do understand and make empowered decisions. Many business owners don't understand the accounting basics and get overwhelmed, so they just take the ostrich approach (put their head in the sand and hope it all goes away!) or just nod along with their accountant and blindly agree with them, not 100-percent sure what is going on.

The truth is, accounting really isn't that hard. Inside my course, The Profit Academy Foundations, I teach profit and money management in an easy-to-understand way. After working it through, many of my clients are surprised how simple it is when you know how.

Make sure you are empowered and educated when it comes to your numbers. After all, this is your money.

Let me break down the basics for you.

BORING ACCOUNTING TERMS YOU NEED TO KNOW

Turnover = Sales or revenue (this is NOT your profit)

Expenses = Costs in your business

Net profit = Sales minus expenses

GST/VAT/sales tax = A direct tax you pay or collect on behalf of the government. This money is not your money. You are simply collecting sales tax for the government or paying sales tax to the government

Income tax = Separate to sales tax, this is the tax you personally pay on money you earn, that is, on the wage or dividends you pay yourself from your business

Company tax = This is the tax a company pays on company profits

SALES VS. PROFIT

Turnover is the total amount of sales or revenue you generate, and it's a completely different figure to your profit.

For instance, one of my clients was an interior designer. When we first worked together, she proudly shared, "I make a million dollars a year." And she was right – she wasn't telling a lie. She did make $1m in sales per year. But she was struggling with cashflow, and when we dived into her reports a little deeper, we realised that she spent around $400,000 on stock and another $400,000 on her team, the warehouse, office and other business overheads. Her actual profit was only $200,000 per year, and she then had to pay taxes out of this amount.

$1,000,000 sales
- $400,000 stock
- $400,000 team, office and other costs
= $200,000 net profit before tax

The truth of her situation was not, 'I make a million dollars a year'; it was, 'I turn over a million dollars of sales a year and make a profit of $200k per year before tax.'

That's very, very different to making a million dollars a year in profit, and, as a business owner, you need to be crystal clear on the difference between the two.

This is a big trend I see in the online business world, where so many people simply focus on their sales or their turnover, without any transparency around the cost invested to achieve those sales. Take this as your friendly reminder not to believe everything you read, see or hear on social media; it's usually filtered through at least one lens, if not multiple lenses!

Online, people can be very quick to celebrate their $50,000 week or their record six-figure month. But they're often not sharing the detail about how much it cost them to get there. They may have generated $50k in sales turnover, but what if they spent $25k in Facebook advertising to reach that figure? What if they spent $60k? What if they're actually running at a loss? And over what time period will the revenue be or has the revenue been received? I know that my first $100k launch sounded very impressive on paper, and it might sound like $100,000 suddenly hit my bank account, but that was for a program that ran over nine months, so the actual monthly revenue was approximately $11k. Still impressive, but puts it in context, right? Is this a consistent result being achieved or a 'best result'? That is, is this person consistently achieving $100k sales months, or are most months $5k with the occasional larger month?

I've also seen people talk about 'making a million' or their 'million-dollar business' and for me – being the accountant I am – I can't help but look at other income figures they have shared. I can quickly figure out that they mean they have made a million since starting their business, which could be over a period of five or even ten years. An impressive feat, yes! But if they're sharing their million-dollar business and implying that it's an annual revenue, not an amount they have cumulatively earned in business, that can be misleading. Not to mention the context of expenses and investments they have made to get there.

The scary thing about this is that many of the people in the situation above don't even know that they're underwater financially. They're so busy focusing on the sales and turnover that they're not paying attention to the running costs and the money flowing out. They're clouded by the noise of the 'success' they're having, and they're not being intentional when monitoring the money they're spending in order to generate that success.

Let's start changing the conversation around profit!

FINDING OUT THE TRUTH ABOUT BIG BUSINESS WINS
(be it yours or someone else's)

- Is this result sales or profit (after expenses)?
- Over what time period is the result calculated?
- Is the result being consistently sustained, or is this a 'best case' result?

GROSS PROFIT VS. NET PROFIT

Gross profit is your total sales less the cost of sales. This is important if you run a product-based business. Cost of sales is the costs that go into providing a service or products to a customer. It is also referred to as cost of goods sold (or COGS). Examples of this are the cost of purchasing products that are sold.

Net profit is your gross profit less the cost of running your business, or your expenses.

As I work mostly with service-based businesses, gross profit is not a term we widely use. I will mostly refer in this book to profit as 'net profit' (that is, your profit after all expenses).

Net profit after tax

Generally, a business needs to pay tax on profit.

If your business makes a profit, you can either:

- pay yourself a wage (and pay income tax).
- distribute the money to yourself some other way, such as dividends (and pay income tax).
- retain the profit in the company (and pay company tax).

The way you pay tax and the amount of tax you pay depends on whether you're a sole trader, a partnership, a company or a trust.

It's very important that you seek expert tax advice specific to your business and your circumstances to work out the best way to structure your business and pay yourself.

The point I'm making is that the profit your business makes isn't the same as the amount of money you can take out of the business and spend.

When you look at your profit number, remember to consider your wage as well. I had a client of mine completely freak out that she'd made $0 profit in a whole year. Then I reminded her that she paid herself a wage of $100k for the year, so while the business hadn't made a profit per se, she was drawing herself a comfortable salary from it.

I often suggest small businesses calculate an adjusted profit that includes the business profit plus the wage they have paid themselves.

Getting from *here* to *there*

Now that we have a clear understanding of what profit is, the next step is to work out how to intentionally grow the profit in your business.

In practice, this starts with some world-class goal setting. It's likely that you're familiar with the concept of setting goals in some way, shape or form, but I want you to really ground your goals in some facts and figures in the form of a budget (in the next chapter, I walk you through this process in detail!).

I don't want this to be the type of book you read once and fail to take any action on it. So, as I mentioned earlier, in addition to loads of case studies and real-life examples, I'll end each chapter with practical tools and tips to help you get from where you are now to where you want to be. These take the form of 'Money Meetings'.

Let me share one of those stories now to show you just how big of an impact it can have to make these mindset shifts around getting right across your money.

When we met, this client was working six, sometimes seven days per week – and she was absolutely burning out.

Her business was based around a low-cost, high-volume product that she produced, packaged and shipped out in-house. She had a full-time assistant, who she paid around $75,000 per year to help her deal with all of the logistics of processing and managing the orders – and business was booming.

She had a successful marketing strategy, and she was generating more orders than she could keep up with.

Turnover was high – nearly half a million dollars per year. But as we know by now, turnover is not profit. When we began working together, I wanted to help her find out exactly how much profit she was making.

She thought burnout was her biggest issue and that financially, she was killing it. But when we dug into the details, we discovered that her expenses were sky-high; her outgoings were growing month on month, and she actually wasn't making that much profit at all.

In fact, she was literally working for less than $900 per week in take-home pay, despite sitting at the helm of a popular, successful multi-six-figure business. She was paying her assistant $75k per year, but she wasn't even paying herself anywhere near the same amount.

This type of situation might be okay if you're in a growth phase. As I've mentioned, some of the biggest businesses in the world don't operate at a profit for many years, as they're focused on internationally growing the business, rather than taking cash out.

If you are intentional about it, have a clear plan to grow your sales and are working towards something bigger, then operating with this type of tight profit margin can be perfectly fine.

But this client? She was in a mature and stable business. We had to do some major reshuffling of her business model and her team to help her build a business set up for long-term success and profitability.

I think I've made my point by now: focusing on just the sales figure can be inaccurate and misleading, especially to you, the business owner.

Getting clear on your profitability is the secret to building on it and increasing your success. How do you even know if you're making more money if you don't even know how much you're making to begin with?

That's why I developed the Intentional Profit Framework and my courses inside The Profit Academy.

The Intentional Profit Framework is a step-by-step process that allows you to really get back to basics and understand the foundations of what your business is all about, while also goal setting and taking intentional next steps to bring about your ideal outcomes in the future.

It's the framework I personally use and the strategy I have used to support clients to double, triple and even quadruple their profitability. It's about having a plan of how to scale. I truly believe the sky's the limit. Your job is simply to decide how high you want to go.

SIX-STEP INTENTIONAL PROFIT FRAMEWORK

This is a six-step process I have developed to help you and your business soar. It guides the growth of businesses and supports intentional decision-making in your business journey. The chapters in this book follow each step in the process, so you have a really clear understanding of the steps and actions you need to take to:

1. Develop an unshakable money mindset

2. Intentionally invest in your growth

3. Anchor your goals within a financial plan

4. Scale up using meaningful marketing strategies

5. Become a gun at pivoting and problem-solving

6. Lay the groundwork for growth and expansion

CHAPTER 2

Key Points

- There's a big difference between sales and profit. Getting close to these figures in your own business is *crucial* – and it's not as hard as you think.

- Understanding the basics of accounting and finances empowers you as a business owner to be in the driver's seat of your money.

- Knowing your numbers is the key to growing your numbers. So, how profitable is your business?

Your Money Meeting Agenda

- **Run your profit and loss reports**
  - » Open up your accounting program and run your profit and loss report month by month for the last 12 months (don't forget to reconcile your accounts first). This will give you an understanding of your total sales for the year, along with your actual profit.

- **Adjust for wages**
  - » If appropriate, calculate an adjusted profit. For instance, if your profit runs at $50,000 for the year, but you also paid yourself a wage of $150,000, then you essentially made $200,000. Also, if you're not sure how to do this, refer to your accounting software guide or ask your accountant for help.

- **Reflect on results and next steps**
    - » Once you have the numbers in front of you, take some time to reflect on these results. Are your numbers in line with what you thought they would be? Are you happy with your current profitability? Are there any surprises?

- **Diarise monthly meetings**
    - » Don't make this a one-off exercise! Every month, schedule a profit and loss appointment with yourself. Keeping close to your numbers is something you should do every single month.
    - » If you need help with the specifics of running all the reports you need to be across your financials, talk to your accountant, or even better, I can teach you exactly how to do this in my course, The Profit Academy Foundations. You can find out more at **www.clarewood.com/intentionalprofit**

Now that you're armed with all of this information, whether you're happy with what the numbers are telling you or not, you have the opportunity to drastically transform your profits. Keep reading, as in the coming chapters, I'll hold your hand through the process of making small but meaningful changes to supercharge your profits.

INTENTIONAL PROFIT

CHAPTER 3:
INTENTIONAL MINDSET

I know you want to be rich.

That's why you picked up this book – because you want to make more profit, right?

There's a funny thing that happens when I make the above statement. People usually have a reaction to it.

Less frequently, the reaction is: "Hell, yeah, I want to be rich!"

More frequently, the reaction reveals a big, fat money story.

A story like: I don't need to be rich to be happy.
Rich people work really long hours.
Rich people are rude and obsessed with money.
Rich people have poor family relationships.

Rich people waste their money on cars and designer clothes.
Rich people aren't charitable and kind.

These are a few of the money stories I've heard over the years, but there are dozens – maybe hundreds! – more.

Think about it for a moment: what was your reaction to that statement? When I say, "I know you want to be rich", what emotion or response does that stir up in you?

It's my firm belief that everyone ultimately wants to be rich. No-one would turn down wealth – why would you? Being rich means you can achieve literally any of your goals and amplify your impact. Who doesn't want to be rich?

The reason people say they don't want to be rich is because they have a potentially negative story they tell themselves about what being 'rich' means. These stories are exactly that: stories. They're not truths.

Even if you don't care about having lots of money in the bank, buying a new car, having a big house or enjoying all the spoils and pleasures that money can buy, there's no scenario in the world where having more money means you can't have a bigger impact in life.

For instance, you might say money isn't important to you and you can't justify wanting more when there are starving kids in the world. Yes, it's appalling that there are children suffering in the world – but you earning less money isn't going to change that.

In fact, the more money you personally earn, the more money you have to put towards the cause that you're passionate about. I believe that if you have the capacity to earn great money, you have the capacity to serve and make an even greater impact. The choice is yours.

Another money story that I hear is: "Money doesn't buy you happiness." And this is certainly true! Money can't buy you love, or connection or fulfilment or happiness.

But having no money doesn't give you these things, either. I would argue that money *increases* your chances of finding happiness, as it allows you to have choices. You can choose to travel. You can hire help around your house. You can afford to go on dates or a dating website. So, while money doesn't guarantee happiness, it can increase your opportunities and capacity to create fulfilling experiences, including being able to give at a bigger level and have a bigger impact on the world. Money buys you choices and money buys you freedom to choose.

The stories I shared earlier about 'rich people' are just some examples of money stories. There are many other beliefs that you might have about money. I'll share more examples later.

Interestingly, while we all have money beliefs, many people don't know what their own stories around money are.

WHAT IS MONEY MINDSET?

Money mindset is your thoughts, beliefs and stories around money. Your money mindset has a lot to do with how much profit your business will ultimately make.

Our stories or beliefs about money can be so strong that we believe them to be a truth. For example, if your experiences to date have shown 'you have to work hard to make money,' it won't feel like a made-up story to you. It will feel like a truth. A fact.

But when you start to work on your money mindset and challenge your belief systems, you can start to recognise that things you thought were an absolute, a definite, a truth are actually how you are *perceiving* what is going on.

I imagine that some children who have grown up in enormous or generational wealth do not have the belief that you have to work hard for money. In fact, they might not believe you even have to work at all. Ever.

One of my ex-boyfriends was from a very wealthy family and he said if we got married – even if we didn't have children – he'd want me to stop working. I said, "What, so I would never work?" And that seemed completely reasonable to him. That's what women in his family and social circles did: when they got married, they didn't work. Something that seemed bizarre to me seemed like the done thing, a truth to him.

Working on your money mindset simply means that you start questioning your money beliefs. It doesn't mean they are all wrong. But it also doesn't mean they are all right. We just start to question those stories and ask, "Is this a truth?" and "Do I want to keep this story?"

Some beliefs we have are very helpful.

For instance, I believe in gravity. If I didn't and I decided to jump off a 20-storey building, that wouldn't end well for me. This is an example of a belief that is rooted in fact.

But I have also had beliefs that did not serve me well. For example, I used to have a terrible fear of public speaking. I still have this fear, although it's gotten better over the years, as I've pushed myself out of my comfort zone and done the work on my mindset to change that belief. I genuinely believed that I would have a heart attack and die if I had to speak in front of a group of people. Any time I had to speak in front of colleagues at work, my fight or flight response would kick in, and I would literally run out of the room. Sometimes, if I knew I had a big presentation coming up, I would take a Valium beforehand to calm myself down. Thinking I would have a heart attack from the anxiety – not a helpful belief – and one I've done a lot of work on over the years!

People think, *When I hit a million dollars a year, I'll feel rich!* They think, *There's no way that someone earning a million dollars a year cannot feel rich.*

I can tell you, I've worked with multiple clients throughout the years who are earning seven figures plus, but they don't live abundant lives. When I hit multiple six figures in my business, I thought my money issues would disappear. But the reality usually is, when your business grows, so do your expenses.

That's why living in the feeling of expansion and abundance, no matter where you are in your financial journey, is so important. It's not connected to the dollar amount; it's connected to how you perceive your life and what's going on around you.

When you live and operate from that expansion, you gravitate towards finding the small ways you can start to level up. It's in the little things: buying fresh flowers for your kitchen, splurging on luxury handwash for your bathroom, or getting that one extravagant appliance you've always wanted, like a Dyson vacuum. It could be anything – whatever it is for you that starts to make you feel abundant.

All of these little decisions lead towards you expanding your mindset to what is possible for you in the future and help you take one step closer to your dream goal. For instance, I had a client who had a dream of living in a house on the beach. Financially, she had shared that this dream wasn't viable in the near future. But I suggested: "Could you go and rent somewhere close to the beach? Even if it's just a one-bedroom apartment? Or could you book a holiday home for a week by the beach, so you can experience the lifestyle and live in your dream for a moment, to see if it's really the goal you want to manifest into happening? Can you get closer to your goal in small but meaningful ways?"

All of the big things I've manifested in my life, I didn't even know how I'd get there. I just would take the one next step I could think of to get me closer.

My big one, obviously, was to build my dream house on the water, within walking distance of the beach. Once I identified this as my goal, I was always thinking: Okay, what's the next step to get me closer? Let's go and see a mortgage broker and see how much money we can actually borrow. Okay, cool. Next step: Let's work out how much deposit we'll need. Great. Next step: let's drive around the area and work out which schools my kids could go to. We drove down to the neighbourhood where I now live several times per month and drove around. We walked through open homes. We would book a night in a hotel that's just a few blocks from my house and walk around our 'new neighbourhood,' sussing out our local restaurants and cafes.

In my head, I was living in my dream suburb much sooner than I was physically *there*. I lived it, breathed it, felt it, experienced it all so vividly that by the time we actually found a home, put in an offer and it was accepted… it felt perfectly natural. Like it was the next step in the journey.

We're in the dream neighbourhood – on the *exact* street we wanted! – and while the home we live in now isn't my dream home, it will be.

EVERYONE HAS MONEY STORIES

Your limiting beliefs around money can show up in different ways and at different times.

I find myself constantly surprised at the money stories that show up for me. There's an extra layer to it for me because this is what I do for a living: I'm a money mentor. Shouldn't I have my shit together when it comes to this stuff?!

Well, that's the thing about money stories: they are always there, always shifting, and they always need attention.

When I look back at who I was ten years ago, or five years ago, or even two years ago, I can see how far I've come and how much I've learnt.

But just when I think I've got it all figured out and my money stories are no longer getting in the way of me creating the best, more fulfilling, most vibrant and adventurous life possible, another lesson shows up to remind me, this is a 'forever' journey.

Where do money stories come from?

Money stories are born out of protection. We build them throughout our childhood and our adulthood based on the different experiences we have, and we develop lots of different coping strategies as a result.

For instance: if your family struggled to pay the household bills growing up and you went through periods of the power being shut off or being behind on the rent or mortgage, you might now have a money story that says: *Household bills are a source of stress.*

I saw this play out with a friend, who would pay his bills the *second* they arrived in the mail. He saw bills as a debt, and he was uncomfortable owing anything. If he received a $1,000 council rates notice with a six-week due date, he would pay it that day. The idea of having that bill hanging over his head for six weeks was impossible to live with.

If you grew up in a household that was financially doing okay, but without much to spare to spend on non-essentials, you might have developed a money story that sees you splurge on life's little luxuries that you feel you were deprived of as a kid. Or perhaps your experiences in childhood have made you even more cautious as an adult and you've gone the opposite way; you now live in fear of 'not having enough,' so you hoard money.

Or if you grew up with financial abundance and never really experienced any financial insecurity at all, your money stories might see you spend a little more recklessly as an adult. You've never known what it's like to truly go without or to decide whether to pay the electricity bill or the rent this week because there has always been more than enough. So, as an adult, you don't save for a rainy day or even save money at all because in your experience, there has always been enough money to go around.

These are just a few really simple examples of the money stories we grow up with, and they can dictate our habits in adulthood. Money stories in and of themselves are just that – stories. But they can become a problem if they hold us back or prevent us from achieving our goals and doing what we really want in life.

The good news: you can work through them and adopt new, better, clearer and more positive money stories. In this chapter, I'll show you how. This is going to be a deep dive into all the reasons you're not getting the results that you want right now. Strap in, because some of this is going to be uncomfortable! It's confronting to realise that one of the major things holding you back has been, well, you.

But it's also going to be enlightening and, I hope, motivating, as you'll discover some of the different habits and beliefs you've subconsciously adopted – and then we can work together to put them in your rear-view mirror.

3 money blocks that result from your money stories

1. Receiving block

This is when you have trouble receiving from others. This block is automatically saying "no thanks" when someone offers you something, whether it's money, resources, a helping hand or a discount. It can also manifest as you not following up to receive the money you're owed.

Our actions are usually underpinned by a story that we have. Here's an example of a receiving block in action.

You're a graphic designer, and a friend asks you to create a logo. They offer to pay, but you have a receiving block and don't want to accept any payment from a friend. It just feels *wrong*. You offer to do it for free, and your friend is thrilled! Which makes you feel good.

Because you're not getting paid, their job falls to the bottom of your to-do list. Understandable – you've got to pay the bills first. It has been two weeks, but you still haven't started. You resolve: first thing Monday, I'll do it!

But Monday comes, and your schedule is busy. You try to get to it all week but by Friday, you have only just started. You set aside half a day Saturday to get it done. Finally, Saturday afternoon, it's done, and you send it to your friend.

Your friend receives the logo and thanks you for your work. But she has requested a few changes: she'd like to see some different colour options, a larger font, and could you flip the image to the other side?

You're frustrated. You worked for free. *On your weekend.* And now your friend is being demanding.

Meanwhile, from her perspective, she was perfectly happy to pay for a logo. She wanted to give you the business – if she's going to pay a graphic designer, it might as well be you. What she wants is a logo she's really happy with, not a logo that's 'good enough'.

This type of dynamic can become a breeding ground for resentment. No-one wins; no-one is happy with the outcome. And it all happens because of the money mindset blocks we're stuck in.

DO YOU HAVE A RECEIVING BLOCK?

Do you:

- Undercharge, or not charge some people at all for your services?
- Do extra pieces of work for free?
- Struggle with boundaries, and overdeliver?

---

2. Holding block

This money block comes up when you are so used to *not* having money, that when you do have it, you repel it.

This type of mindset can be the result of financial instability in childhood or as a young adult, and your subconscious instinct is to repel money.

We often have an amount of money that we feel 'comfortable' holding. For some people, they love to have $50,000 in their business account at all times 'just in case'. Whereas others are used to having a maxed out business credit card at all times. Take a moment and reflect – what bank balance is the amount that you tend to gravitate back to?

In business, a holding block can show up as a similar compulsion to spend when we have more than what we are used to. For instance, I've seen an example of someone who suddenly increased their income in a short period of time. She felt so uncomfortable with her new-found wealth that she found multiple ways to spend it – and quickly.

She jumped into a ton of courses she never actually opened or attended, went on an extravagant overseas holiday, bought a bunch of designer clothes and handbags, bought a flashy new car, and basically got rid of the money as soon as possible.

I'm not saying you shouldn't enjoy your money or reinvest in your business. But are you spending that money intentionally? Or are you repelling the money because you're not used to holding it?

DO YOU HAVE A HOLDING BLOCK?

Do you:

- Struggle to keep any money in your bank account?
- Spend money as soon as it lands in your account?
- Feel unworthy of having any sort of buffer?

3. Spending block

A block in spending is when you struggle to spend money – either on your business, or in your personal life.

This shows up when feeling uncomfortable with outlaying money. In a business sense, this might look like a fear of investing into the business. For example, not hiring a new team member, or joining a course that could help you with your business.

In your personal life, you might scrimp in certain areas. For example, you might feel really uncomfortable buying nice linen or towels.

This block can be really unhelpful where it holds you back from growth in your business, or in your personal life where it limits your enjoyment when you have the money to spend.

I shared earlier in the book how investing in a coach impacted my immediate profit. At the time, I was earning $12,000 per month, and $7,000 of that was profit.

I made the scary decision to invest in a coach at a cost of $3,000 per month. This obviously reduced my profit immediately. But it was ultimately an investment that paid off: within a few months, I started earning an average of $25,000 each month.

My profit grew- to up to $17,000 per month – and that's after subtracting the investment in coaching!

Someone with an spending block would have been happy to continue profiting $7k per month, without making the investment, and they may have missed out on the potential epic growth as a result.

> **DO YOU HAVE AN SPENDING BLOCK?**
>
> **Do you:**
>
> - Have a mentality of "I can do it myself"?
> - Refuse to invest in courses or resources that could help your business?
> - Scrimp and save, and only feel safe with a big cash buffer?

There's no right or wrong answer in terms of how much you should be receiving, spending or holding. The real question is: are you consciously aware of how you are behaving around money and why?

HOW TO DEVELOP AN INTENTIONAL MINDSET

Being clear about exactly what you want is crucial. It's the first step towards creating your dream outcome – because once you know what you want, you can work out how you intend to get there.

This is why creating a plan or budget is very helpful in breaking through your money blocks. Rather than flailing around and either not spending a cent or spending way too much, you can see the effects on your growth of not spending (or spending too much). It's very important through your planning process to keep checking in on the stories you are telling yourself.

For example, someone with a spending block might say: "I can absolutely double my sales, without investing a cent into coaching, marketing or building a team." This might be true. But if we accept this as a truth without investigating it, we could be limiting our growth and failing to step into massive opportunities.

The more we identify, recognise and work through our money stories, the more we are able to receive, hold and spend with ease. To do this, we should:

1. Create a money plan.

2. Check in constantly on WHY you are making decisions.

3. Ask if the story you believe is still serving you.

4. Create your new (more positive) story about money.

I want you to think for a moment about some people you know who are wildly successful. These are the type of people who always land on their feet, who have luck on their side, who seem to keep smashing their goals, and life only gets better and better.

Look at them as an example of what is possible in your own life and ask yourself: *Why can't I do it?* If you notice limiting beliefs start to pop up around why you can't achieve a similar result, challenge your thoughts or stories.

For example, I know a coach who took three months off and travelled overseas to completely focus and write her business course. Was I envious? Hell yeah! Did I notice my money stories bubble to the surface? You bet I did!

Well of course she can write a brilliant course and have a big launch if she has three whole months to do it, with no kids, no housework, no distractions and no work getting in the way, I thought.

Then, I noticed the thought.

Paused. Reflected on it.

Recognised that the story I had created didn't particularly serve me, as it implied any course I created couldn't possibly be as good as hers because I didn't have three months and no distractions to write it.

So, I threw away that thought.

I energetically congratulated her on a job well done and celebrated her success. I reflected on her opportunity and realised how much I'd appreciate some clear, focused time in my own schedule to work on my course, and then I made that happen.

Being intentional is *not* about sitting around singing 'Kumbaya' and manifesting and trusting that the things you want will magically land in your lap. It's about determining what you want and creating a plan to achieve it, while being open to things showing up in a different way to the plan.

It's a practice I continually undertake in my own life, and I see the results of it. When I respect money and open myself up to the possibilities and opportunities, money comes back to me.

This is the power of an intentional mindset: it can lift you out of negative, muddy thinking and up into a space of endless opportunity and growth.

CHAPTER 3

Key Points

- Your money mindset is often subconscious, and it can sabotage your growth and success.

- There are three main money mindset blocks: receiving, holding and spending.

- Many people fall for the 'I'll be successful when...' myth. You can live in a success mindset *now*! There's no need to wait.

- Developing an intentional profit mindset is *crucial*. When you're clear about your dream outcome, you can work out exactly how you intend to get there.

Your Money Meeting Agenda

- **Identify your money stories**
    » Spend some time and reflect – what are your stories around money? A good place to start is to put pen to paper and journal: "What are all my beliefs about money?" While you are writing these out, explore, "Where has this belief come from?" It's incredible when the pieces of the puzzle start to fit together, and you realise you have ABC beliefs because of something that happened in your past.

- **Recognise your money mindset blocks**
    » Identify what your main money block or blocks are – is it in holding, receiving or spending? We all have one, and we can

hold two or even three! Figuring out what these are can help you then work out how to stop letting these blocks hold you back.

- » Get intentional by brainstorming and writing a list of things you could do differently to break through those blocks. For instance, if your money block is spending and you're the type to scan a menu for the cheapest possible meal, set yourself a task of eating at a restaurant and ordering a more expensive meal. Small but powerful shifts will help you nudge your mindset in the right direction.

- **Build an intentional mindset**
  - » Start to catch your negative beliefs about money. When you find yourself thinking an unhelpful thought around money, reframe it to be a more positive perspective.
  - » Pay attention to the words you use out loud around money. For example, if you say, "I can't afford that" reframe it to, "I'm choosing not to spend my money on that right now." If you say, "Oh that will probably never happen," reframe to, "I can't wait until X happens."

Need help reframing your thoughts into a more positive outlook? Download my free 50 Money Affirmations at **www.clarewood.com/intentionalprofit**

CHAPTER 4:
INTENTIONAL INVESTING

"You've got to watch your expenses."

"Don't spend too much on your business."

"You want to spend how much on a course/training/coaching?! What a rip off."

If you run a business, then odds are you've heard or said one of these phrases – or something similar – at one point or another.

We're very conditioned as business owners to keep an eye on our expenses, and this isn't a bad thing. It's smart – you need to be across your numbers.

But here's the truth of the matter. If you don't invest in yourself and your business, it's almost impossible to level up. You can't make big, bold strides forward in what you're trying to achieve if you're playing it safe and sticking well within 'known' parameters.

I want you to take a second and think about a huge, successful company or business owner who you admire. It might be a single person, a brand, or even a really big multinational company. Think for a moment about their trajectory: do you believe they achieved all of their success because they did everything the 'right' way? Do you think they broke through new boundaries, created new and innovative ways of doing things, and achieved massive, unthinkable goals because they continued to do things the way they'd always been done?

Not likely.

I can share my own experience as an example of this. If I were to wind the clock back a decade or so, I could have made the decision to keep going with my accountancy career. Let's say I had my kids; then I went back and picked up my career exactly where I left it. What would my life look like?

Well, it could look pretty good. I'd be climbing the corporate ladder. I'd be earning good money. I'd probably be working long hours. I'd rush out of work at 6 pm and battle peak-hour traffic to race home and take over from the babysitter, who has already ferried my boys around to sports and activities and bathed them and fed them dinner. I'd tuck them into bed and kiss them goodnight. And overall, everything would be... good.

Is that what we want out of life? Is that what you want? A life that could be described as 'good'?

That's not what I want.

I want an extraordinary life. Unimaginable success. Outrageous, insane, 'I can't possibly begin to think what it would be like to live like this?!' levels of happiness, health, connection, love and wealth.

That's the kind of thinking that got me into my light-filled waterfront home in a beautiful coastal city. It's what has helped me launch and grow my business into a multi-six-figure – soon to be seven-figure – company. And it's what I'm going to use to help you have that same level of success.

PLAYING IT SAFE VS. PLAYING IT BIG

One of the reasons why people succeed in life is because they don't play it safe.

They dream big. They imagine, plan and strategise, and they take calculated risks.

And none of this happens without an investment: an investment of time, energy, money, planning and more.

You'll notice that I use the word investment rather than the word expense. This is not an accident. It takes a real mental shift to change your outlook, but there's a reason why I've changed the language that I use from my accounting days, back when I used to be far more comfortable labelling costs as precisely that: costs.

Why have I changed my tune?

When I first started my business, I set it up lean.

L-E-A-N.

I bought my first logo for $99 (I literally cringe when I think about it!), and I built my first website myself on a platform called Wix. As someone who isn't gifted in the artistic department, let me assure you I did not have Apple knocking on my door asking if I could design their next website.

With my disgusting website and embarrassing branding, I was waiting for clients to bang my door down. I stumbled across a business coach, and he was charging $1,000 per month. It seemed INSANE to pay anyone that much when I had zero income, but I had such a strong sense about it that I hired him. Within one month of working together, I had signed my first private coaching client at $1,000 per month. I kept on plugging away and signed several more.

Pretty soon, I was making $5,000 per month revenue, paying my coach $1,000, and had almost no other expenses. So, I ended things with my coach, and my profit was almost at $5,000 per month (less a few small expenses).

Genius! Accountant Clare kept her costs lean and her profit high.

I ticked along like this for a while, and I found signing new clients relatively easy. Business was good.

But then something happened. I started to notice a few other coaches who had started their business at the same time as me talking about their results. And they weren't playing around doing $5–10k months. They were making multiple-six-figure revenue – and even shooting for the seven-figure mark.

I started to wonder… *what were they doing differently to me?*

I took off on a snooping mission and noticed that they were hiring expensive coaches. They were joining masterminds. They were attending conferences in America. They were creating content continually and had podcasts and fancy websites and flashy branding.

I had a big 'aha' moment. I could either keep playing it safe and keep achieving the same results – results that were good but not extraordinary – or I could put my big girl pants on and spend some money, with absolutely no guarantee that it would pay off. But with the possibility that it could pay off, big-time.

I knew I wanted big things. I had a hunger for a business that was wildly successful. For the big coin.

I could stay safe, or I could take a risk and lean in.

And lean in, I did.

Some of my investments were incredible game changers for me and my business's growth trajectory. I joined a mastermind and within a few months of joining, there was a massive shift, and I almost doubled my revenue overnight.

Other investments were slow burners. And some were downright duds.

But every time I leant in, I either learnt a valuable lesson (don't do that again!) or had a big uplevel.

What shifted in the most meaningful way was that regardless of the outcome, there was momentum, and it was forward momentum.

That was when I realised that playing safe was playing small.

I was recently asked a question about my coaching clients. When it comes to those clients who I have worked with to help them achieve massive income leaps, what are the common threads or common actions?

In other words: "What do the people who get the best results actually do?"

And I answered: "They lean in! If things work out, they celebrate and progress. If things don't go to plan, they don't sulk and blame others. They take the learnings, jump back on the horse again and keep charging forward. They are so clear on their desires and their destiny that literally nothing will stop them."

THREE QUESTIONS BEFORE MAKING ANY INVESTMENT

1. How much money do you ACTUALLY have to invest?

There is a big difference between feeling uncomfortable with an investment and literally not having the money and having to take out a loan.

2. What is your appetite for risk?

I know some people who have literally taken out an additional mortgage on their home or a credit card to invest in a program/opportunity (I personally wouldn't do this, but I know it has felt right for some people!). Your risk appetite might depend on your age, your money mindset and your 'what happens if it all goes wrong' plan, which leads to:

3. What is your contingency?

If this investment all goes pear-shaped, what is the 'get out of jail' plan? For example, if this investment doesn't go to plan, I have a nest egg of $20,000 in savings I can use to bankroll my business until income picks up, or I will get a part-time job in my industry until I get my feet back on the ground.

FOUR TYPES OF BUSINESS 'INVESTMENTS'

Which ones are the 'right' investments to make in your business, and when should you make them?

Well, I'm afraid to say it ain't black and white. Any of these might be clever investments for you, but others won't make much sense at all.

To begin with, it's a good idea to get clear about the different types of investments you can make into your business and what they mean. As you read through this list, consider where your biggest investments might be at the moment and where opportunities may exist.

1. Overhead costs

These are costs that support you to run your business. They won't necessarily add more revenue into your business but will free up your bandwidth and create more ease. These include:

- Email marketing tool
- Website maintenance
- Accounting and bookkeeping
- Subscriptions
- Admin support
- Office expenses

2. Revenue-adding investments

These are investments that you anticipate will generate more sales in the short-term. These include:

- Hiring a business coach.
- Joining a mastermind or online program.
- Investing into marketing, for example, hiring a Facebook ads manager.
- Building and growing an email database.
- Enrolling in sales training.
- Building and streamlining the customer journey/funnel.

3. Brand investments

These are investments that you make that will help you build your brand to create more opportunity and brand visibility. They don't necessarily drive sales immediately, but they will lead to growth over time. These include:

- A beautiful logo and brand identity.
- Creating a podcast.
- Hiring a public relations (PR) agency.
- A slick website.
- Brand photography and videography.

4. Cost reduction investments

These are investments that are not sales-driving, and they represent ways to reduce your business expenses long-term. They may involve an upfront cost but will save you money overall. These include:

- Investing in a consultant to optimise systems.
- IT programs and platforms with an upfront cost.
- Hiring a permanent staff member instead of contractors/freelancers.
- Working with a consultant on your organisational structure.
- Paying admin/junior staff to research if there are more cost-effective alternatives available for certain expenses in the business.

INTENTIONAL INVESTING IN PRACTICE

You usually know what you need to invest in to get to the next level. If you aren't sure, there is an activity to help you unlock this at the end of this chapter, in your money meeting activity. Now the next thing to consider, if you know what you would invest in, why are you not doing it already?

I've worked with people at various stages of their business, and I've helped them move through that feeling of 'if I had'.

For instance, 'If I had a full-time marketing manager, I could increase my sales by 200 percent'. The mindset here is stuck around thinking that without a marketing manager, they'll never enjoy the sales bump they have their eye on.

My suggestion? How about we flip that to: I want to increase my sales 200 percent. Therefore, I should invest in a full-time marketing manager!

It's only a small rephrase, but it's powerful because it places the intention of the outcome and the power around that decision firmly back in your hands.

So, let's assume you've recognised that hiring a marketing manager is the way to go. What happens next? Usually, we fall into a bit of 'but' conversation.

Your 'but' is your reason why you haven't yet taken action.

But... I don't have enough spare time in my calendar to take time away from the business to look at hiring someone.

But... what if it doesn't work out and I'm stuck with a dud employee who I have to let go?

But... I don't have enough money to take that step and actually commit to hiring someone.

But... what if there are no good marketing managers out there and I waste all that time, with nothing to show for it?

But... I've hired someone before, and it was a total disaster!

We each have our own 'buts' (or your money story, as I spoke about in chapter two). This is where we revert back to that process of identifying the story we tell ourselves and then investigating: What's the truth? Is this story serving you? Or is it holding you back?

Over the years when I've encouraged my clients to invest in their intentional investing journey, it (often) pays off for them in some way in time. Here, I want to share a few examples of this.

A big one that many business owners can relate to is the fear around the step of investing in a new staff member, especially if it's their very first employee.

One client of mine was always flat out. Busy, busy, busy. She had enrolled in my mastermind program, as she had a very high demand for her services, but she was a one-woman show, and she was struggling to keep up. It was obvious she needed to hire some staff – the business was screaming out for structure and support.

"What's the big thing holding you back from hiring someone?" I asked her.

"I know I need to bring someone into the team," she said. "But… what if business slows down? What if I lose a few customers, and I'm stuck paying a team member that I can't afford?"

We workshopped it as a group. For those who have never been involved in a mastermind before, it's a really collaborative, supportive environment where we all work together as a team.

So, we all jumped behind her and said: "Go for it! It's time. You've got a bunch of people lining up, wanting to work with you. You're already madly successful. If you've already got a queue of people ready to buy your services, imagine how many more sales you could generate once you have extra support and your time is freed up to invest into marketing and growing your business?"

So – she hired her very first team member. Then a few months later, she hired another team member as well.

Inside the time she spent enrolled in my mastermind program, she doubled her revenue from $20,000 per month to $40,000 per month. Since then, she has been able to leverage her time to show up in her marketing and social media like a total boss, which has led to even more sales.

This is the power of intentional investing.

Another one of my clients had a successful business, and she wanted to attract an even higher calibre clientele, who would pay a higher price point for her services. She was creative, and her service was in a creative industry, where price points vary from very cheap and cheerful to absolute top-of-the-line.

I was straight up with her. "You can absolutely level up your offering, offer a premium service, and charge a lot more than you do right now," I told her. "But you can't elevate into attracting the right kind of high-end clients with your current brand."

I found someone to help her reimagine her brand and come up with a whole new brand identity. This branding specialist wasn't the cheapest option on the market. In fact, she was probably one of the more expensive.

More expensive does not always mean better – but sometimes, it does. Sometimes, it denotes experience and expertise.

My client was as nervous as hell about making this investment. She knew she could find someone cheaper.

"Sometimes it makes sense to find someone cheaper," I said. "But you want to attract really high-end clients who spend five figures to engage you and your service. That means you need to have a beautiful, high-end, high-quality brand. You can't cut corners here – you need to invest in this."

Could she have achieved the outcome of a new logo and branding more cheaply? Absolutely.

Would she have received the same level of quality and then had the same confidence about her business, her brand and her opportunities to grow with a more affordable substitute option? No way.

The knock-on effect of this confidence can't be underestimated. It radiates out of you, the same way that a flawless blow-dry will have you sashaying out of a hair salon.

She could not have achieved that result with a cut-price designer. There's also a psychological element that happens when you intentionally invest in something. You feel proud and confident, and that translates to how to show up in your business.

She was proud to promote it and share it, and that led to more and more conversations, which led to more business. Her business became far more profitable and once she began attracting the higher calibre clients who were paying a premium price point, she was able to deliver less work and charge more for it.

She ultimately was making a bigger profit margin – all because of one strategic, intentional investment that well and truly paid off.

For my client, her investment in her branding transformation resulted in her making more profit – and that's possible for you, too.

> **WHAT IF YOUR INVESTMENT DOESN'T PAY DIVIDENDS?**
>
> You're not always going to get it right. But it's my genuine belief that every failure or misstep gets you closer to success.
>
> If you try something and you fail, at least you are moving – it's better than staying stagnant. I've failed a thousand times over in my business, and I know I'll fail again in the future.
>
> You learn lessons from the loss, adapt, and evolve for the future.

YOUR NEXT STEP

By now, you're getting clear on the possibilities that exist when you have a clear plan for intentional investing. There are a few things you can do from here to work out what to do next.

The first thing that most people do is: dive into their worst-case scenario.

Some people gravitate towards focusing on the worst possible outcome (a reminder that these money mindset stories can show up in all sorts of ways!). This is known as a negative bias. Our brains are literally programmed to focus on negative over positive as a survival mechanism.

For some of us, it can feel really comfortable and familiar to first consider: what's the worst possible thing that could happen?

"If I hire a staff member..."

→ It's going to cost me so much money.

→ I'm going to have to earn $XX just to break even.

→ I could hire the wrong person altogether.

→ It'll put so much pressure on my bottom line.

→ I'm gonna potentially lose so much money.

The flip side of this is: how much more could you make? If this is a dream hire and the person drops seamlessly into your workflow, what could that mean for your profits? What if your business income doubles? Where your attention, focus and energy flows, your results follow.

If you have a tendency to 'catastrophise' rather than searching for the potential positive outcomes, here's my suggestion.

First of all, recognise that 'worst scenario' thinking is often layered. It's like an onion, with the ultimate core fear buried in the centre before being wrapped in a dozen layers of other fears, concerns and considerations.

Start with your worst-case scenario.

I hire someone for one day a week but make no extra money this month – in fact I make less money than usual.

Okay, so that means you've got less money coming in, but you've got bills to pay and money pouring out of your business account.

What happens next? Work through that.

I have to dip into my savings this month to pay my business bills.

What happens next?

My savings account is going to be $3,000 lower after I've moved this money to my business account.

What happens next?

It happens again. So I'm facing a second month of less income and higher expenses.

What happens next?

If business is slow, this is a massive opportunity. If you don't have as many clients as usual, you'll have plenty of time to double your marketing efforts, show up more on social media, perhaps even reach out to your database with a special offer.

What happens next?

I make some extra money, but less than I need to cover the wages of my new staff member.

What happens next?

I contact a couple of my suppliers and request a two-week extension on my due dates. And then, I strategically use that time to get out there making offers, marketing and making sales.

The reason I like this 'what happens next' strategy is because when you do it, you often get to the bottom of each problem and then realise: I can problem-solve this. I can live with the outcome. This is not the end of the road, because I can get creative and find a solution.

And if you can't? If it is the end of the road and you can't see one possible solution in front of you that doesn't lead to a poor outcome, what can you do?

My therapist once said something to me, which is really relevant to this discussion. She told me: even if something transpires and it is the absolute worst-case scenario outcome, it is happening anyway.

Spending three months worrying about it won't change the outcome.

But focusing on what you can do puts your head back in the game. It means you're showing up the way you need to be for your clients and your family and your relationships.

Flip your thinking: what's the best-case scenario?

You've hired a new team member for one day per week and because you have an extra set of hands, your revenue grows by 20 percent in the first month.

The following month, it grows a further 30 percent, and you increase your new employee to two days per week.

Within a few months, you've bumped them up to full-time, and you've doubled the amount of revenue you were making before hiring them.

This type of outcome is totally possible. I know, because I've seen my clients achieve it!

Whether you're the type to always think of the worst-case outcome, you're a dreamer who believes absolutely anything is possible, or you fall somewhere in between, whatever your mindset and belief system, there's something I want you to try.

Right now, think about an investment you've been considering. It might be a big investment, like hiring a full-time staff member. It could be something on a smaller scale, like hiring a virtual assistant for two hours per week.

Whatever it is, if you're even considering the investment, then you must believe – on some level – in the possibility of a really fantastic outcome. Otherwise, you wouldn't consider it in the first place.

Take this particular investment and consider… what's the absolute best thing that could happen?

CHAPTER 4
Key Points

- If you want to have epic leaps in your profitability, you need to invest in your business. It is very unlikely you'll create huge, meaningful, life-changing results unless you're willing to invest along the way.

- Not all investments pay off – however, some of them do, big time. And you'll never have the chance to experience massive growth and achieve your dreams if you don't try.

- If an investment like this isn't possible in the next 12 months, what smaller investments could you take along these lines? Add these to your budget so you can start to step into the space of intentional investment and growth.

Your Money Meeting Agenda

- **Identify how you would like to invest in your business**
    » If you were handed $100,000 'no strings attached' tomorrow and you had to invest it in your business, what would you spend it on? Write it out and allow yourself to get excited about what could be possible.

- **Work out how much to invest**
    » Now that you've 'dreamed big', work out your realistic next steps. How much do you have to invest – and are you willing to invest – in your growth in the next 12 months?

- **Identify your mindset stories around investing**
  - » Journal in response to the question: "Why am I scared to invest in my business?" What are you afraid will happen? What's your idea of the worst-case scenario, and why are you focusing on that instead of the best possible outcome?

- **Map out your next steps to prepare for your budget**
  - » If you can't go 'all in' on investing in the next 12 months, what are the smaller steps you would like to take to move forward? For example, if the ideal is to hire an in-house Facebook ads manager and spend $50k on Facebook advertising, you could invest in a course to learn Facebook ads yourself and set aside $500 per month for ads in your budget.

INTENTIONAL PROFIT

CHAPTER 5:
INTENTIONAL PLANNING

In the last chapter, we worked through money stories and the power they can hold over us when making decisions big and small.

Next, I want to touch on 'comparison-itis'. We're all familiar with this: comparison-itis is when we compare ourselves to others and to our perception of their success, their relationships, their lifestyle, their wealth, and so on. It can be a real challenge when it comes to your money mindset and the success you ultimately have.

Let me share a quick story about a friend of mine.

One day, she was scrolling on social media, and a series of beautiful landscapes filled up her feed. It was a post from an old colleague, who had taken a family holiday camper-vanning around New Zealand.

There was lush greenery, stunning cliffside landscapes, and a picture-perfect young family splashing about in the water. There were campfires and toddlers giggling while they toasted marshmallows and by the time she'd finished scrolling a couple dozen photos, my friend felt those familiar micro-feelings wash over her: Jealousy. Envy. Desire. Craving.

She wasn't genuinely envious of this friend. But she was instantly struck with the idea that maybe she and her husband should plan a trip around New Zealand? A camping and caravan adventure? With their three young kids?

When she told me this story, she was laughing. "I hate camping," she said. "I don't like long drives. And I can think of nothing worse than being locked up in a campervan for two weeks with my kids whining, 'Are we there yet?' the whole time."

What she recognised in that moment was that comparing herself to someone else was prompting her to pine for things that she didn't even really want.

This happens to all of us on a daily basis, and I notice it constantly when I'm coaching my clients about setting goals for their businesses. We see the results or outcomes that other people are achieving, and it warps our perspective. It steals our attention and has us focus so much on what they're doing and achieving that we lose focus on what it is that we really want.

This is what intentional planning really boils down to.

What do I actually want?

It's not: what I think I should want.

It's not: what someone my age or in my industry should want.

It's also not:

- What my parents or family believe I should do.
- What social media hypes up as 'success'.
- What society tells me I should want (the white picket fence isn't for everyone!).
- What others around me tell me matters the most.

It really, truly is so individual, and it is so closely tied to your money stories because those money stories lay the foundation for what you truly desire.

The good news, as we explored in the last chapter: your money stories can change. Therefore, your goals can change. They can become bigger. Bolder. More exciting. More outrageous!

As we dive into this chapter and explore intentional planning, how do we make sure you're really and truly working towards what it is you actually want?

"You can't create what you don't allow yourself to desire."

> ## THE COMPARISON TRAP – OR OPPORTUNITY FOR INSPIRATION?
>
> While one part of living your most intentional and profitable life means working out what matters to you, you also want to get clear on what doesn't matter to you. It's all too easy to end up comparing ourselves to others and coveting what they have.
>
> If you notice that flicker of envy or jealousy pop up when you see what someone else is achieving, creating or doing with their life, ask yourself... does what they have really excite you on a soul level?
>
> If your answer is no, send them energetic, good vibes and move on with your day. If the answer is yes, then congratulations – you've just identified a new goal!

WORKING OUT WHAT YOU WANT

When I do this exercise with my clients, it's fascinating to see the stories that come out. I did this at a retreat, and I asked all of the participants what they really want.

Some people come back with a realistic goal – perhaps a little bit of a stretch goal from where they are now, but something quite achievable.

"I want to make $200,000 this year, I want to buy a slightly bigger house, and I want to have $20k in savings."

Then there are the ones who are shooting for the stars.

"I want a ten-million-dollar home in the most exclusive suburb in my area. I'll have a three-storey house with a lift and floor-to-ceiling glass with views of the ocean. I work only ten hours a week and have a staff of cleaners, cooks and household helpers to help me achieve my goals. My family and I take business class trips to Europe every year, and we have a holiday house in the south of France."

Both of these lines of thinking are valid; there's no real right or wrong here. But here's the thing about the second example. She doesn't just have this as a goal; she sees it as a vision. She believes this lifestyle is hers. Not just in the future, but now. She can expand to living in the vibration of being a multimillionaire with a multimillionaire lifestyle. She believes she's worth it and she deserves it and every day, the decisions she makes take her one step closer to realising this vision.

When you're in an expansive mindset, you gravitate towards opportunities. You have the confidence to say yes to invitations and experiences that you previously may have declined because you thought you weren't ready yet or didn't have anything to offer because your business was small.

For some of you reading along right now, you're thinking, *This is bullshit*. And I totally acknowledge this! Because I used to feel the exact same way.

You can't just 'manifest' wealth into being. You have to do the work, right?

Absolutely.

And that's why this work is so powerful. Because it's about combining:

The right mindset

+

Positive money stories

+

Work, persistence and drive

=

Achieve your true potential

Your true potential is literally anything you want. There is no limit.

You might be rolling your eyes, like, righto, sounds good. But how does this actually work?

The thing is, I know this is totally possible. Because I've experienced it myself. I've seen it happen for others.

And I want you to believe that anything is possible.

Consider this: if you are reading this book and have freedom, access to running water, food in your pantry and a roof over your head, with access to wi-fi, then you are in a position of privilege.

In his book, *The Barefoot Investor*, Scott Pape shared some staggering statistics. This was in 2017, so the average wage has changed a little since then. But at that time, according to the Australian Bureau of Statistics (ABS), the average Australian earned $78,832.[2]

If you earn this much or more per year, you are in the top 0.28 percent of the richest people in the world.

In other words, if you earn the average Aussie wage, you're richer than 99.72 percent of the global population.

I'm going to challenge you and say that a big part of what is holding you back from achieving your wildest dreams is your own mindset, your own self-limiting beliefs, which can get in the way of creating the life that you want.

Working out what you really want in life is not a 'set and forget' type of thing. You might decide that right now, what you really, really want in your lifestyle is a nanny or babysitter for certain periods of the week to help manage your small kids while you build your business. Once the kids are at school, you might realise, *I don't really need a nanny anymore. But what could really change the game would be a housekeeper to help keep on top of our home chores.*

Or you might dream of living the laptop lifestyle, travelling and having new experiences, until one day, you get sick of unpacking the suitcase again and again and just crave a stable home.

You should keep checking in on those desires, and that includes checking in on your goals, desires and dreams in your business.

Does the work you do still light you up? Are you attracting the right kinds of clients? Are you enjoying the work you're doing on a day-to-day basis? Are you stressed and overwhelmed and working long hours, or do you have a solid semblance of work-life balance?

WHAT IF YOU REALLY CAN'T AFFORD IT?

Let's talk about the elephant in the room.

It's all well and good for me to make all of these suggestions about outsourcing, getting support and setting yourself up for success. But many of these suggestions have a cost attached – and what if you genuinely, absolutely, really cannot afford them?

I've been there. When I first started out as an entrepreneur, spending $35,000 on a new website and branding was completely out of the question, but that's the sum I invested in 2022.

It was also only about five years ago for me when the idea of paying for a babysitter was literally not an option. Now we have a nanny who comes four times per week and does the school pick-up each day.

So, what did I do back then when I didn't have the budget to intentionally invest in the things I wanted to do? And what's my advice to you if you're in the same situation now?

Start where you are.

If you really don't have the money and you're just starting out in your business and you don't have a wealthy partner, swollen bank account or rich family to fall back on, then look at the things you can do to help you achieve your goals.

Think of it like this: let's say you wanted to go to Fiji for a holiday. If it were an ideal, 'dream' holiday, where you're wealthy beyond your wildest dreams, you'd fly there business class, get picked up by your private chauffeur-driven limousine, check in to your five-star resort with stunning views and enjoy a sensational five-day trip, with a private chef and a luxury tour guide.

However, your budget right now is more Jetstar than private jet. You can still find ways to enjoy some luxurious experiences along the way, though.

You could look for ways to get lounge access at the airport before your trip (some credit cards offer free lounge access) so you can toast the trip with a glass of bubbles at the airport before take-off. Check to see if you have enough frequent flyer points to upgrade to business. Or you could book one super-special, five-star dining experience – or do some research online to find luxury accommodation at a discount.

Or perhaps going overseas isn't even an option. How can you create beautiful and luxurious experiences in your life now? Before we could afford a babysitter, my hubby and I would pop to the shops in the afternoon and buy some yummy cheeses and wine. Then once we'd put the kids to bed, we'd light a bunch of candles, lay out a picnic rug on our lounge room floor and put on some romantic music. Those have been some of my favourite date nights!

My point is: there are options! So start where you are to add luxury, abundance and expansion to your life.

When I was a 19-year-old, broke uni student, a group of girlfriends and I sat on a bus and travelled from Brisbane to Thredbo for 20 hours. My suitcase was half-filled with two-minute noodles, and I ate them for lunch and dinner for five days straight. By day six, I was craving something else, and we went out for dinner. It cost $35 for a steak and veggies, and I just about died when the bill came, as that was a big chunk of my spending budget for the whole trip gone.

But at that point of my life, that's where I was at. I intentionally invested in that extravagant (to me at the time) experience, and I still remember it to this day.

Wherever you're at – invest at that level. Don't make yourself sick by investing in things that push you so far out of your comfort zone, you can't sleep at night.

Expansive baby steps

This can mean being creative and taking 'baby steps' like:

- Arranging childcare swaps with friends and family. You have your friend's kids Tuesday this week; she has your kids Tuesday next week. You both gain a full day kid-free to work on the business.

- Asking for alternative ways to engage in a service. Let's say you identify a service that could uplevel your income, but the cost is out of reach right now. Contact them and ask if you can pay for 1–2 hours of personal advice instead of enrolling in a full course or program. Topics could include Facebook advertising, social media marketing, Canva training, public speaking or media training.

- Enrolling in group training. If private one-on-one coaching with your favourite mentor is a goal, but it is out of your price range right now, enrol in one of their more affordable group programs.

- Boosting your income in other ways. There is no shame in having a second job or a side hustle on your side hustle while you grow your income.

- Service swaps. Some people are very 'anti' this concept but if there's an energetic match, it can be a massive win-win. For instance, you're a graphic designer, and you design someone's brochures and business cards; they're a copywriter, and they provide you with the copy for your new website. I have done masterclass swaps with other coaches, where we share audiences. As long as it's an even swap and it's a fair exchange of time and resource, this can be a game-changer.

HOW TO TURN INTENTIONS INTO REALITY

It's all well and good to have your dreams. But you can't just sit on your backside, hoping and wishing that money will come flying into your bank account.

This whole practice and philosophy of intentional planning is grounded in reality. You've got the dreams; now, you need to create the roadmap to get you from where you are now to where you want to be.

This type of introspective yet 'big picture' thinking is where having a coach can be so valuable. As I've mentioned, I've invested a lot of money in my own coaches. I know I can spend this sort of money on a coach because I have a really clear budget and clear forecasts.

I also know that the investment I make in my coach is what pushes and drives me to set outrageous goals and then knock them out of the park. I have someone I'm accountable to, someone who has a vested interest in my success. Without my coach helping me to set stretch goals – and then checking in regularly to make sure I'm actually working towards them – I don't believe I'd achieve half as much as I do.

Most small business owners (my guess is 95%) don't set a budget. When I ask "why", they often say:

"It's too confusing and overwhelming, and I don't know where to start."

"What's the point? I have no idea where my results are going to land, and what if I get it wrong?"

"I don't have time."

Maybe these excuses resonate for you? Here are some compelling motives to set a budget for your business:

- Clarity about your direction.
- A month-by-month breakdown of the revenue targets to achieve to hit your big goals.
- Mapping out your investments by month.
- A benchmark to track your progress against, to keep you on track to ensure the business profit targets are achieved.

There's a reason why big businesses all set budgets… because this process works.

If you do happen to have a business budget – fantastic! This next section will help you refine and build on it. And if you don't, these steps will get you on the right track.

5 steps for building an effective budget

A budget is a plan of what you intend to earn and spend. It can be over any period of time but for the purposes of this book, we will be working on a 12-month basis from the date that you do the exercise.

Step 1: Start forecasting your revenue

The first step is to forecast what you expect to earn, month by month, for the next year.

The easiest and most effective way to do this is to split it out into categories of where that income is going to come from. For example, you might have one category for project work, one for courses, one for consulting work, and so on.

> **Hint:**
> Don't limit your possibilities by using your previous trading history as an indication of how much you can expect to make in the year ahead. That's a very traditional, accountant mindset, to consider your past performance as the best indicator of your future performance.
>
> Instead, have a think about what you would like to be earning in each month and what would be possible if you really 'went big' in your business! Could you launch new revenue streams? Do you want to increase your prices? What could you achieve if you invested in working with a coach, hired a team member or spent more on your marketing?

Don't get too hung on up on your sales forecast. You might not know exactly how many students are going to join your course or how many clients you'll have. Your forecast numbers are just educated guesses, using the best information you have at the time. Your budget is just a roadmap, or a guide.

A budget doesn't have to be perfect! Things are going to change. You might miss your revenue targets, overspend or underspend. Think of your budget as a guidepost to track your progress against. The process of forecasting gets easier the more often you do it!

> ## CASE STUDY
> ### Revenue Forecast
>
> Let's say you own a digital marketing agency. Before you create your forecast, have a think about your top-line objectives for the year.
>
> You will aim to:
>
> - Start with five clients on retainer, paying $3,000 each per month. Then add two additional clients every second month.
>
> - Offer consulting, aiming for three consulting calls per month at $1,000 each. The price will increase to $2,000 after six months but only stay at three calls.
>
> - Launch a course in March, making $24,000 revenue.
>
> - Launch a second round of the course in September, making $48,000 revenue.
>
> Then put it into an excel spreadsheet. It's as simple – and difficult! – as that.

INTENTIONAL PLANNING

Example Case Study Spreadsheet

		Jan	Feb	Mar	Apr	May	Jun	Jul	Aug	Sep	Oct	Nov	Dec	Total
RETAINER CLIENTS	Number	5	5	7	7	9	9	11	11	13	13	15	15	
	Price	3,000	3,000	3,000	3,000	3,000	3,000	3,000	3,000	3,000	3,000	3,000	3,000	
	Total	15,000	15,000	21,000	21,000	27,000	27,000	33,000	33,000	39,000	39,000	45,000	45,000	360,000
CONSULTING	Number	3	3	3	3	3	3	3	3	3	3	3	3	
	Price	1,000	1,000	1,000	1,000	1,000	1,000	2,000	2,000	2,000	2,000	2,000	2,000	
	Total	3,000	3,000	3,000	3,000	3,000	3,000	6,000	6,000	6,000	6,000	6,000	6,000	54,000
COURSE	Number			12						24				
	Price			2,000						2,000				
	Total			24,000						48,000				72,000
	Grand total	18,000	18,000	48,000	24,000	30,000	30,000	39,000	39,000	93,000	45,000	51,000	51,000	486,000

Step 2: Forecast the costs for your team and wages

One thing I've noticed with my clients is the 'chicken or the egg' element with hiring. You might think: I want to get to XYZ stage, then I'll hire the person. Or, When I'm making this much money, then I'll hire support.

But this is where you get to be truly intentional. A lot of the time, the chicken does come before the egg. You need to ask yourself: How much am I willing to lean into what feels good to me? How am I being intentional with the direction of my business? Do I have the financial bandwidth to invest at this stage?

Hiring someone before you might feel technically 'ready' can work as a motivating force. For other people, the idea of hiring someone before there is more than enough work for them can make them feel sick to their stomach. It's all about aligning your risk profile with your action. If you want to take a tiny amount of risk, that's fine, but you'll likely end up with a smaller result.

This comes back to your mindset and intentionality, because when you plan and spend with intention and you link investment to outcome, you can quickly see if something is working or not – and then quickly pivot as a result.

If you have an existing staff member or you're planning to hire in the future, it's crucial that you calculate your ROI (Return on Investment). If you're spending X amount per year on a part-time employee, are they helping you achieve at least that value (plus their expenses) in additional sales and revenue (less tax)?

Add their salary and any other on-costs. Don't forget to include insurances, equipment including computers, superannuation/ 401k, subscriptions they will need, plus any travel costs and other incidentals, for example, if you buy birthday gifts for team members.

Remember, you don't necessarily need to hire people on a permanent basis into your team. You can use contractors, freelancers and employees on a casual basis if you aren't ready to commit to permanent wages. Usually, contractors will cover their own on-costs, and their fee will be all-inclusive, but it's worth checking the law in your country and their contracts.

Either way, map out the team costs month by month and add to the expenses in your budget.

Step 3: Consider other expenses

Run a profit and loss report for the last 12 months and after reviewing your expenses, do some analysis. Through this process, you'll determine which costs should be carried forward in your next year's plan. This is important because people often forget what their regular business expenses are. For example, you might underestimate just how much you spend on subscriptions or contractors.

As you review, consider:

- Is each area of spending essential and important?
- Are you going to get a solid return on investment from the spend?
- Do you want to intentionally continue spending that money in the next year?

It's my belief that there's a strong correlation between the sales you want to achieve and the investments you're willing to make.

Many people want to take small, low-risk steps and get big results – but it doesn't work like that. If you want to think and achieve like a six- or seven-figure business owner, then you need to adopt the mindset of a six- or seven-figure business owner.

If you want to achieve a different result, then this is the time to do things differently. I get that it's uncomfortable, but as someone famously said: "Insanity is doing the same thing over and over and expecting different results."

Make sure your spending aligns with your purpose and goals. When I'm sitting with someone and prompting them as we go through this process, I ask questions like:

- What if you were to double the income you earned last year?
- What if there were no limits on your earning potential?
- What would you invest in to get those results?

This does not mean throwing money around and spending willy-nilly. Nor does it mean that you can't make money without making huge investments. However, I really believe that the fastest way to get big growth is to invest – in the right things, at the right time.

How much this is, and in what areas, and the timing of it will vary depending on your stage of business and your capacity to invest. Again, this comes back to being very intentional. What is the intention of spending this money, and what do you expect the outcome to be?

INVESTING IN QUALITY VS. OVERSPENDING

How do you know how much to invest into certain areas? Where should you invest in quality and where are you just wasting money?

I love a bargain. Who doesn't? But there are certain things in life you shouldn't scrimp on – seafood, your hairdresser and certain areas of your business.

When working out where to spend vs. where to save, come back to:

→ **Who your ideal clients are.**
What are their values? What matters to them? You're not going to attract the type of high-level clients you want with a free website you designed on Wix – I can give you that tip!

→ **What pricepoint you're operating in.**
If you sell a $100 course, you're probably not going to send someone a bunch of flowers to welcome them to the course. But if you sign up an ongoing client for six months, then you might.

→ **What your personal values are.**
This comes down to areas you perceive as a commodity (important, but at the best possible price) vs. expertise investments (where paying more can leverage better results).

Once you have mapped these out by category and month, you can add these into your budget.

Step 4: Consolidate and create a profit projection

This is where the rubber hits the road on your budget. You take the revenue projected in Step 1 and outline the expenses projected in Step 2 and 3, month by month. Then you put it all together in a spreadsheet and work out if you're making a profit (remembering that profit equals sales minus expenses).

Here is an example of what a profit projection could look like:

> **CASE STUDY**
> **Profit Forecast**
>
> We'll continue forward with the case study from earlier – a digital marketing agency.
>
> You have already forecast the revenue, so you can copy those amounts across to the profit spreadsheet.
>
> Next let's look at expenses. For this example, let's add in:
>
> - A big growth in the team costs from July (with a plan to have a huge sales month in September) and a plan to increase director's wage from July.
>
> - Flat costs for contractors, accounting and subscriptions all year.
>
> - Facebook ads, increasing budget from July.
>
> - Costs for coaching and copywriting, with increases across both expense categories.
>
> Now that you have captured all budgeted expenses, add these into your spreadsheet.
>
> You then calculate your monthly profit or loss by subtracting your expenses from the sales.

Example Case Study Spreadsheet

	Jan	Feb	Mar	Apr	May	Jun	Jul	Aug	Sep	Oct	Nov	Dec	Total
Sales	18,000	18,000	48,000	24,000	30,000	30,000	39,000	39,000	93,000	45,000	51,000	51,000	486,000
Expenses													
Accounting	500	500	500	500	500	500	500	500	500	500	500	500	6,000
Team wages	2,000	2,000	2,000	2,000	2,000	2,000	10,000	10,000	10,000	10,000	10,000	10,000	72,000
Director wage	6,000	6,000	6,000	6,000	6,000	6,000	10,000	10,000	10,000	10,000	10,000	10,000	96,000
Contractors	1,000	1,000	1,000	1,000	1,000	1,000	1,000	1,000	1,000	1,000	1,000	1,000	12,000
Subscriptions	500	500	500	500	500	500	500	500	500	500	500	500	6,000
Facebook ads	700	700	700	700	700	700	1,400	1,400	1,400	1,400	1,400	1,400	12,600
Coaching	1,000	1,000	1,000	1,000	1,000	1,000	3,000	3,000	3,000	3,000	3,000	3,000	24,000
Copywriting	500	500	500	1,000	1,000	1,000	1,000	1,000	1,000	1,000	1,000	1,000	10,500
Total expenses	12,200	12,200	12,200	12,700	12,700	12,700	27,400	27,400	27,400	27,400	27,400	27,400	239,100
Profit	5,800	5,800	35,800	11,300	17,300	17,300	11,600	11,600	65,600	17,600	23,600	23,600	246,900

You might be making a little bit of profit. You might be making a lot of profit. Or you might be making no profit at all. Sometimes, you might choose to intentionally run your business at a short-term loss while you invest in growth and scale.

For example, in the calendar year of 2021, my business made $370,000 revenue. My business was still quite profitable, but my profit margin was lower than usual, as I intentionally invested heavily back into the business. These investments included a high-end business coach, full new branding and website, and researching, writing and publishing this book.

I shared the full details on my podcast (episode 157) if you want all the nitty-gritty but in a nutshell, I was prepared to make these investments because I had intentionally planned and budgeted for them. They weren't decisions I made on a whim; they were strategic decisions made about a short-term investment that would deliver results over the long term.

When you look at your profit projection, are you happy with it? Do you need to move things around? Are you aligned with the overall picture?

PLANTING SEEDS

Consider: What goals are on your list for the next 12 months, 2 years and 5 years – and what seeds do you need to plant (investments do you need to make) to get the ball rolling?

Step 5: Formalise your plan

It's also a good idea to sense check your projection with an accountant so you can be sure you've crossed all the t's and dotted the i's. You will also forecast the amount you will draw as a wage or distribute to yourself as a director or owner. You should also forecast tax based on the budget, including personal tax and/or company tax and add both of these into your plan.

The final step in the process is to add the budget into your accounting program. This is going to help you create some powerful reports so you can review your progress against your budget every month and make sure your plan is on track.

Your accounting software will have a section that says 'budget'. You can load this information up into your accounting software; then your budget becomes your living, breathing framework to see if you are sticking to your plan. Every month when you do your monthly Money Meeting review, you can check your actual performance against your plan.

If the plan isn't on track, that's okay! These steps are not set in stone and if you don't hit your projected targets, that doesn't mean you've failed. It does mean you have new information to work with, and you can re-adjust your goals, your spending and your plans accordingly.

As you monitor and review, it can highlight the lack of action you might be taking. It could even highlight that the plan was all wrong! And you might need to go in and revisit and tweak it, over and over again.

When you go through this process of intentional planning, you run a fine line between thinking and dreaming big, and grounding those dreams in reality. This is where some of those pesky money stories can show up and try to take you down. If you notice yourself falling back on familiar thought patterns that tell you 'you can't', 'you won't', or 'you're not good enough', revisit some of the money mindset strategies we outlined in chapter three – and knock them on the head.

Need more help?

This is a pretty high-level snapshot of how to create a budget. If you need more support to create your profit plan, you can ask your accountant to work through this process with you, or you can join my course, The Profit Academy Foundations.

Inside my course, I go through the budgeting process step-by-step, and I share a spreadsheet you can use to make the process really easy (plus there is much more inside this course to help you master your business finances). You can join my course at **www.clarewood.com/intentionalprofit**

When budgeting your expenses, analyse each item and ask – "Is this contributing meaningfully to the long-term profitability of my business?"

CHAPTER 5

Key Points

- The first step in intentional planning is working out what you truly desire in your business and in your life… and then creating a clear plan on how to get there.

- The next step is to work out how much you are able and willing to lean into the intentional investment strategy you have mapped out.

- Now that you've got your goals, it's time to work out the step-by-step practical actions to take next. For example, if you want to double your revenue, you might need to launch a new offering, which means you need to hire a new team member or contractor.

Your Money Meeting Agenda

- **Identify what you really want**
    - » Grab your journal and write in response to the following questions. Write without judgment on what comes up:
        - › What do you really, really want?
        - › If anything were possible and if there were no limits, what would you do, be, experience or create?
        - › Think about this in every area of your life: your business, your relationships, your family, your social life, your health and vitality, your hobbies, your income, your working hours, your achievements… the list goes on.

- **Convert your dreams into your next 12-month budget (aka action plan)**
  - » Map out your revenue plans. What sales would you need to achieve, month by month, over the next 12 months?
  - » Forecast the team costs and your own wages and add these to your budget.
  - » Add any other costs to the spreadsheet.
  - » Consolidate and calculate your month by month profit forecast.

- **Formalise your budget and create a plan to track your progress**
  - » Ask your accountant to review your budget and to forecast your taxation.
  - » Upload your new budget into your accounting program.
  - » Each month in your monthly money meetings, have a look at how your actuals vs. your budget are tracking to check how you are progressing against your plan to make sure you are on track towards your big goals.
  - » If you're not hitting the goals and targets you've set, don't despair. There are plenty of levers you can pull to boost your income. We'll get to those in our marketing chapter.

CHAPTER 6:

INTENTIONAL MARKETING

Now that you've got the mindset of exponential growth, what do you actually do to make more money?

The best, easiest, most impactful, practical way to make more money?

It's by marketing your business!

But before you dive in and start dancing on TikTok and taking out billboards on the side of every major road in town, it's important to step back and think about: 1) the mindset of marketing; 2) being intentional with your marketing strategy; 3) nailing your branding and messaging.

What do I mean when I say the mindset of marketing?

The reason why I speak so much about mindset is because it is the foundation of action in any area of your business. If you just 'take action' without the shift in beliefs behind it, then the things that you DO, you won't do consistently.

Let me explain the **Be – Do – Have** model.

Most people say: I want to **Have** XYZ outcome, so I'm going to **Do** XYZ action.

But first, you need to **Be** who you need to be first.

Let me explain.

I was coaching a client who was really struggling with the concept of 'showing up' on social media. In her particular business, her social media strategy was a key driver of new business, so it was essential that she showed up – regularly, consistently, authentically.

She would go through spurts of posting things for 2–3 days at a time, but then she'd completely drop off the radar for a week or two, sometimes even more. She would Do the thing she needed to do, but she hadn't fundamentally shifted her identity to become who she needed to Be in order to achieve her goals.

"It's all about consistency," I told her. "If you're serious about growing your brand and connecting with your audience on social media, it's really important that you show up regularly."

"But it's so hard!" she said. "I don't know where you get all of your ideas – how do you show up and post every single day?"

Here's the thing: in the beginning, it was really hard! I had imposter syndrome, it felt very unnatural, I hated showing my face on social media, and coming up with ideas was like pulling teeth.

But I did it anyway. I was consistent and I found that the more I did it, the more natural I became at speaking in front of a camera. Then, ideas began flowing more easily, and sharing content became second nature to me. In fact, these days, I love to post on social media, which is why I do it so often!

The same feelings arose around my podcast. When I first started recording episodes, I felt like a total fraud. In fact, I was so uncertain about the value it offered that I almost didn't even launch it.

Thank God I did, because my podcast launched at number two on the business charts for Apple Podcasts in Australia and as of today, The Clare Wood Podcast has delivered hundreds of episodes and reached a global audience that has wildly exceeded my expectations. Most importantly, it continues to accomplish my marketing goal of connecting with new people and generating new potential clients.

My point? The more consistent I am with my marketing, the more consistent my results are.

I had to **Be** who I needed to be first (consistent, confident, and always ready to show up and try my best) before I could **Do** the thing I wanted to do (create a podcast and grow my social media profile) in order the **Have** what I wanted (a bigger social media presence that drives more customers).

I don't just 'do' posting on Instagram in a race in the lead up to a course launch. I consistently add value to my audience almost every single day. (Psstt, if we aren't already connected on Instagram, please come on over and give me a follow @clare_wood_coach).

To be honest, I don't even think about my marketing that much anymore. I am a content creator – it's how I identify. I'm always thinking of ways I can share money tips to help my audience, not just when I have something to sell.

I've shifted into the identity of being a business leader who 'does' things on autopilot. I show up as a next-level business leader because that's who I am.

This is what I mean when I say 'Be' the kind of marketer you want to be, rather than just 'Do' things you think you need to do in a burst.

I'm not necessarily saying you need to be on Instagram every day, nor starting a podcast (we'll get to marketing strategies later on). But what I am saying is that you need to think about your marketing funnel – whatever that looks like – as a continual thing that your business does on autopilot, rather than a tap that you switch on and off when you feel like it.

I recognise that this sounds overly simplified. "Sure Clare, I'll just suddenly start creating a ton of content every day."

So, I want to remind you of this.

Shifting into the state of Be happens through the discomfort of Do-ing.

I used to hate to show my face on social media. I cried for months and months on end when trying to build up the confidence to record myself talking on camera. But I kept on moving forward through the discomfort. Because I knew that on the other side of that discomfort was the next-level version of myself – it was who I needed to embody in order to take my business to the next level.

Whatever marketing strategies you want to employ in your business, start small. Start consistently. But just start.

And keep on going, pivoting direction if needed.

MARKETING IS THE BACKBONE OF YOUR BUSINESS GROWTH

Even the biggest, most well-known brands in the world, such as McDonalds, Coca-Cola and Apple, still invest into marketing consistently. Why? Because you can't attract new customers and continue to engage with and retain your existing brand and clientele if they don't know what you do and how you can help them.

Now that you have the 'Be' marketing mindset in place, what the hell do you actually 'Do' in terms of a marketing strategy? Well, here's the good news and the bad news. There is no one marketing strategy that is right for every business. I can't give you the silver bullet that will make you an overnight millionaire (I wish I could!). But there are some marketing foundations that will apply to you, no matter what kind of business you run.

Introducing: your marketing funnel

Every business needs some sort of marketing funnel. That's simply a marketing phrase for: a process of reaching potential customers who previously didn't know your business and turning them into paying customers.

The reason it's shaped like a funnel is because it's likely people will drop off at each stage. You don't expect every person who ever hears about your business or brand to buy from you. In fact, you plan for the fact that some of them – or even many of them! – won't.

So, from first hearing about you, some potential clients will immediately drop away. Perhaps they don't need what you are offering, or they aren't in a position to afford it. Or maybe you're just not the right fit for them? This happens, and it's perfectly fine!

But some of them will continue to be interested and intrigued by what you offer, so you want to move these potential clients through your funnel. Some clients might skip phases of the funnel – for example, they might find a Facebook ad, jump straight in and buy something without doing any research about your business. So, they skip building trust, connection and interest and jump straight to buy. But generally, most customers will follow this process, so it's important you get familiar with each step.

What does this look like?

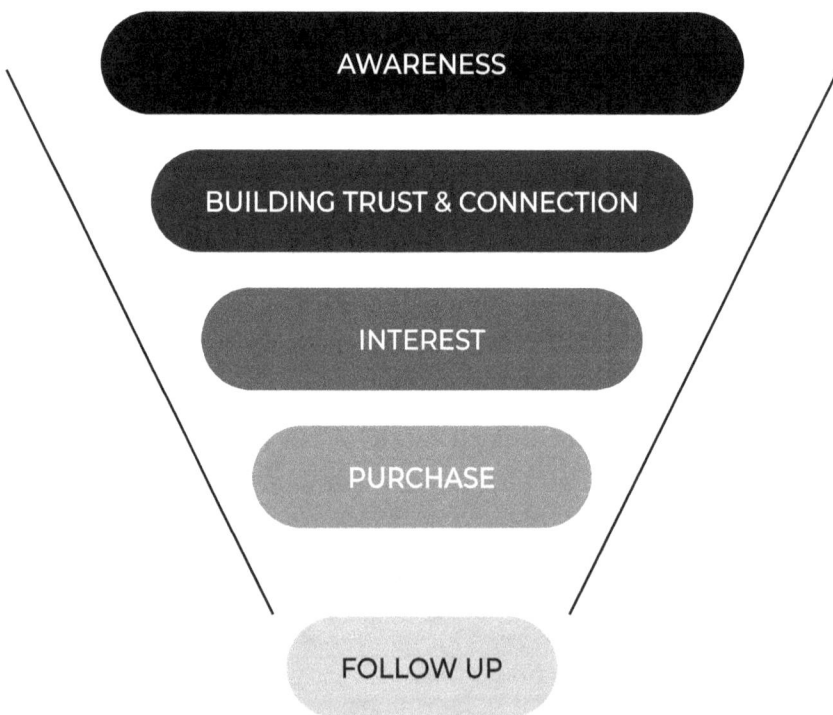

Awareness: is the top of the funnel of your marketing strategy. This is the part of the marketing funnel where potential clients first find out about your brand, through marketing, advertising or word of mouth.

Building trust and connection: is where you are piquing a potential customer's interest in your brand through content, testimonials, reviews and developing a relationship.

Interest: is when a potential client starts expressing a desire to learn more about working with you by reaching out.

Purchase: is the time when a customer says, "Yes! I want to buy from you." This step also includes what that experience of purchasing from you looks like for them.

Follow up: is the experience that a customer has after they buy from you.

Let's discuss each element in more detail.

Awareness

How do you know which awareness tools are right for your brand?

As I mentioned earlier, there is no 'one size fits all'. It will completely depend on your business.

My biggest tip here would be to think about your ideal customers. Where are they hanging out? How can you tailor a marketing strategy to them?

When it comes to how many top-of-funnel marketing activities you should have, this really depends on the size of your business and your bandwidth to deliver content across these channels in a meaningful way.

However, it is essential that you have multiple top-of-funnel strategies so your business isn't reliant on any one channel for success. Instagram could go under. Your referral opportunities could dry up. So, it's important that you have several ways for finding new clients. As a guide, I'd recommend for a small business to have (at least) five top-of-funnel marketing activities they regularly undertake.

EXAMPLES OF BUILDING AWARENESS:

- SEO (finding your business organically via Google)
- Paid Google ads
- Social – Tik Tok, Instagram, Linkedin, Facebook, Twitter, Pinterest
- Referrals/word of mouth
- Paid social media advertising
- Networking events
- Presenting at events
- Print media
- Public relations
- Influencers

Building trust and connection

Gaining awareness of your brand and offering is one thing but once you have people's attention, you need to ensure you can keep it. This boils down to education and communication, which is where you focus on growing the relationship and developing trust.

It's pretty rare that someone sees your business for the first time and purchases straight away. Even with a low cost investment, many people will check the Google or Facebook reviews before committing.

Depending on the price point of your services, it might take longer before people feel confident to invest to work with you. So, how do you bring someone from not knowing your business to purchasing from you? Through building trust in a process called **Know – Like – Trust**.

This process is about sharing more about your brand, your offering and what your clients have to say to see if it's a fit for this potential client.

Before you sell, you want to add value. If every post you share online and every communication you send out in your newsletter is a pitch for a sale, you're going to lose your audience.

To build a community and genuinely interact, you need to offer value – and to do that, you need to give people a reason to come and learn from you.

This is why I always ask my clients in my programs: "How are you adding value to your audience today?"

If you're helping people solve problems and you're adding value, you're building trust and giving people a reason to seek out your expertise. Then, when you ask for the sale, the money will flow.

> **EXAMPLES OF BUILDING TRUST AND CONNECTION:**
>
> - Social media content that entertains and adds value
> - Blogging
> - Social proof, testimonials
> - Customised communications
> - Checklists, guides and templates that add value to your community
> - Regular newsletters with valuable tips and information

Interest

At this stage of the funnel, someone has expressed an interest in working with you. The three key things to do next are: 1) make it easy for people to work with you; 2) have a really clear, simple and straightforward sale process; 3) develop a simple and ethical process to finalise a sale.

Your golden principle here is to make it easy for people to work with you. How many times have you visited a website to get more information on a brand or company and afterwards, you're even less clear on the service they offer or how you can actually work with them? It happens so often, and it's usually because people are so busy trying to explain what they do instead of explaining how they can help their potential client solve their problems.

For instance, there's someone I follow online. I love her work, love her vibe, and I've always felt drawn to working with her. One day, I felt called to reach out and find out more about her offering.

I clicked on the link in her Instagram bio, and it went to a landing page for an offer of group coaching, which I wasn't interested in.

I then Googled her and searched around her website to see what services she offered. I was keen for one-on-one sessions but after digging around her website, it wasn't really clear:

- What types of one-on-one sessions she offered (One-off? A series? A timeframe?).
- What her packages were or what the pricepoints were.
- Whether she was taking on new clients or fully booked.

So, guess what I did? Nothing.

I was a hot lead, but she never got my business. All those hours spent marketing her top-of-funnel on Instagram didn't convert to an interested potential customer because she wasn't making it easy for people to work with her.

How much business are you missing out on because you fail to make it easy? Because you fail to follow up? Because you fail to check whether your contact links are working, your marketing is clear and you're accessible to your audience?

Once you've made it easy for people to interact and shop with you, you need some strategies in place to close the deal. Some deals and sales will happen effortlessly, seamlessly… and for others, sales skills really come into play.

This requires you to look at everything, from the small (do you have a process in place to respond to email enquiries and direct messages on social media?) to the big (do you have a clear and defined sales process that encourages and invites people to buy from you?).

Some tips for closing the deal:

- **Ask questions:** Seek to understand their pain points, then demonstrate how you can solve them. Or get to know their pleasure points and show how you can help them achieve these. Either way, stay focused on them.

- **Seek permission to share:** "Would you like to hear how I could help you with that?" If the client says yes, it's a soft mini-commitment, and it creates space for an open conversation.

- **Share the solution:** If this client signs on with you, what changes can you help them bring about? How are you going to help them level up? How are they going to feel after the transformation you support them with?

> **Bonus Tip:**
> If you're confident you can help someone who has enquired with you, then why should you feel bad about sharing your price? Don't focus on the fact that you're asking them for money, but focus on what you're giving them in return. Confidence is key. If you don't feel confident, remember – you have something to offer that is going to help them. You can solve a problem or fulfil a need.

> **EXAMPLES OF POTENTIAL CLIENT EXPRESSING THEIR INTEREST:**
>
> - Asking questions
> - Interacting on social media
> - Asking for a price list
> - Requesting a meeting or call
> - Clicking on your website

Purchase

The next phase in the process is the actual purchase phase.

The purchase phase is where the customer actually takes the leap and buys your product or service! How does the process go from their perspective? Is it easy and effortless for them to buy from you?

How do you welcome them into the experience of working with you? Do you thank them for choosing to work with you?

A friend of mine recently bought an online course. She took the big step and purchased! She had that post-buyer's wobbles/remorse that can pop up after a purchase. *Did I do the right thing?* she wondered.

She waited and waited and didn't even receive a receipt for the purchase, let alone an email with the next steps.

Three days passed, and she wondered, *Did the transaction go through?* She checked her bank statement and yep – it had. She was left feeling deflated and disappointed in the customer service experience. And, as most disappointed customers do, she didn't complain, but she told all her business friends about the experience.

Once a client has made the commitment to buy, it is important to reassure them they have made a great decision. And of course, to deliver them an excellent experience with your brand.

EXAMPLES OF HOW YOU CAN CREATE A PREMIUM PURCHASE EXPERIENCE:

- A welcome gift
- A thank you email outlining "next steps"
- Confirmation of the purchase and a celebration that they have chosen to invest
- A handwritten card
- A phone call

Follow up

Follow up is such a critical phase in the sales process, yet so many business owners forget to nurture their customers or clients.

It's believed that it costs roughly seven times more to acquire a new customer than it does to sell to an existing customer, so it makes sense to develop a strategy to look after your current clients as part of your sales funnel.

Relationships are so important in business, and your customers will love to feel valued and appreciated.

The easiest way to create a consistent post-sales experience around follow up is to have a system in place. For example, at the one-week mark after purchase, they receive an email; three months later, a check-in and an upgrade offer; six months later, another email, and so on.

This can be automated or diarised so you don't forget to undertake these steps.

In today's day and age of TikTok and iPhones, people have a shorter attention span than ever. We forget about businesses and brands unless they are in our face on a regular basis, and it helps to be the front-of-mind brand that regularly reaches out to check in.

EXAMPLES OF A FOLLOW UP:

- A survey to ask about your client's experience
- Offering them an offer on a renewal, rebooking or subscription to retain their business
- Surprise and delight gifts; for example, birthday gifts
- Suggesting an upgrade of services
- Reaching out to them personally to chat about their experience with your brand and asking if they have any friends who might need your services
- Asking for a testimonial or review

"Let excellence be your brand. When you are excellent, you become unforgettable."

– OPRAH WINFREY –

BRAND VOICE AND MESSAGING

The final step in the marketing process is nailing your branding and messaging.

This is not a marketing book, so this certainly isn't a comprehensive guide, but I wanted to share a few top-line tips to help you make more money.

It starts with the question: how do you uncover what your brand voice actually is?

Do this exercise to start to get an understanding of what you and your brand are made of.

Ask the following questions:

- What is a 'word bank' that describes you and what you do? Ask, what are things you would never say? For instance, I'd never say "babes" or "boss babes"; it just doesn't align with the way I personally speak or interact.

- And then ask, what are some things you always say? For me, it's money, profit, success, transformation. These are the pillars of my business!

- What are your core values?

- How are you and your brand different from your competitors?

- What do you want your brand not to be? For example, do you inspire people gently or motivate through brute force?

You could also ask other people, such as a partner, business friend or previous clients, how they would describe you and your brand in three words.

When you get clear on your brand voice, you can harness the power of storytelling in a really meaningful way.

A great place to start when working through this is: What's the history and the background of what you do? What drives you to do what you do? Why did you launch your product or service in the first place – who are you trying to serve or help?

Were you a new parent struggling with a certain area of your life, and that pushed you to launch a new product or service around parenting? Do you have any stories about your customers or clients you could share to reinforce the impact you have?

If so, unlock and share those stories with your community. It's not always about generating sales. In fact, the quickest way to burn your audience is to sell to them in every second post. These stories can come from anywhere and can be anything from small processes you use to work through to big, life-changing, 'aha' moments you've had.

A lot of business owners focus on sharing their own success stories, and I also love to share my clients' wins and achievements. Sharing the transformations, stories and experiences of your clients can be a powerful way of connecting and adding value without selling. Nothing inspires me more – and it inspires my followers, too.

You can also educate your audience by sharing behind the scenes snippets and glimpses into your life and business. People can be inspired by your success, by your creative process, by your relationships. Depending on your brand and your audience, you might draw inspiration for posts from your travels, your lifestyle, your habits, your home, your clothes, your cars – the list is endless.

For instance, I get a lot of engagement on my social media posts when I share holiday snaps or photos from events and retreats. I know a copywriter who gets great engagement from sharing little tips and tidbits for others when creating their own social media posts.

As another example, I once worked with a copywriter who shared with me that before she starts working on a project, she always listens to a set playlist. She cultivates a playlist for her client customised to get her in the mood for creating for that brand. I suggested she share this story on social media. It's a great way to connect with her audience and tell stories about her process.

The idea is to share stories, insights and ideas that help people feel more connected to your deeper story. So, what is your brand's story?

What are the stories you can tell about your brand?

- **How** did you build your business?
- **Why** do you do this work?
- **When** are you available to work with people?
- **What** exactly does your business do, and what outcomes do you help people create?
- **Who** do you want to connect with? Who do you want to attract?

How can you weave real-world stories into value-add examples for your audience?

This chapter was written to take the mindset work you did earlier and convert it into some practical marketing strategies to add dollars to your bottom line.

I've shared a number of tips, tools and techniques in this chapter, so hopefully you're overflowing with ideas and actions now, and you're feeling pumped about HOW you can grow.

CHAPTER 6

Key Points

- Marketing is an essential part of building a more profitable business.

- When it comes to your marketing, as always, it starts with mindset and understanding any fears or limiting beliefs you have holding you back from taking action. Once you understand your mindset and take steps to align it to your next level of success, you can implement marketing strategies to skyrocket your profitability.

- The final part of the marketing process is to take your growth mindset and convert it into action, using a marketing funnel as a reminder of your overarching strategy.

Your Money Meeting Agenda

- **Identify your marketing mindset.**
    » Do some journaling to the following prompts:
        › How do I currently behave with marketing in my business?
        › Am I a business that adds value and shares offers with my audience, or am I holding myself back?
        › How does the next level version of me behave around marketing?
        › Who do I need to Be in order to step into my next level of growth, and what do I need to Do to support that?

- **Create your marketing funnel.**
  - » Want to uplevel your marketing? I've created a marketing funnel template for you to populate to help you build your marketing plan from the ground up so you can identify strategies for finding new clients, building Know, Like and Trust with them and turning them into paying clients. You can download this for free at **www.clarewood.com/intentionalprofit**
  - » Identify any gaps between where you are and where you want to be. Write an action plan to put those steps in place.

- **Do an audit on your branding and messaging.**
  - » Do you have a clear idea of your ideal clients and a clear brand voice to target them?
  - » Is your branding and overall marketing and positioning clear and consistent?
  - » Do you use storytelling in your messaging?
  - » Create an action plan to fill the gaps you currently have in your branding and messaging and set reminders in the calendar to check your progress against your plan.

CHAPTER 7:
INTENTIONAL PROBLEM SOLVING

Running your own business isn't always smooth sailing. In fact, sometimes it's downright crap.

In truth, the good parts, the bad parts and the downright ugly parts? They are actually all good parts. Even the hard bits. Even the really, truly challenging moments. Even the cry yourself to sleep at night, 'Why is this all so hard, God I wish I was anywhere else but here' moments.

These are the moments that truly shape us as human beings. They help us create resilience and grit, and they prove to be a fertile breeding ground for learning – learning what we don't want, what doesn't work for us, and what steps we could take next time to avoid ending up in the same position again.

In my experience as a mentor, I've seen hugely successful female entrepreneurs fall in a heap because they're facing a particular challenge that is bringing them to their knees. Sometimes, it's a really big issue that's stopping them in their tracks. Sometimes, they've just had a slow month or quarter, and they're struggling with motivation, or they're out of ideas on how to turn it all around.

In the following pages, let's dig into some of these challenges, and I'll share some of the strategies that I've used personally in my own business and that I've helped my clients to deploy in their businesses to overcome the challenges and move forward with passion, purpose and profit.

But first, I want to set the record straight on one so-called 'challenge' that I hear about all the time and that I'd like to try and shift your thinking around. It's a challenge that my clients and social media followers bring to the table regularly; we discuss it in our masterminds, debate it in my DMs, and I've had numerous discussions about it at retreats, conferences and events.

The challenge is growth – and the concept that growth needs to be linear.

Newsflash: growth isn't a straight line upwards.

Think about the property market. When you buy a house, depending on when you buy it in the market cycle, its value in the future will change. It could grow in value if the market booms or decline in value if the market cools. For the most part, a property's value coasts along, neither growing nor falling, until the next 'trigger' in the property cycle.

Running a business can be very similar. Businesses move in cycles, too.

It begins with the startup phase, where you run everything on the smell of an oily rag. You do everything yourself to save money; you service every possible client who walks in your door, and you run yourself ragged trying to get the business off the ground so you can enter your proof phase.

The proof phase is where you figure out if the business really has legs. Can it operate and drive a substantial profit without you becoming a burnt out husk of a human being after working 16 hours a day, six days per week to make it work?

If it passes this test, then you move into the growth phase, which is all about investing into the business to scale up. This is the part of the journey where most people expect the successes and the growth to be linear, and that's usually not the case. In fact, as I regularly remind my clients and I'm now sharing with you: it is completely normal to have periods of stagnation or even contracting profits as your business grows.

We have a misconception in the filtered world of social media that our business needs to grow month on month and year on year and if that's not happening, then something is 'wrong'.

In reality, it is extremely rare that any business grows and grows and grows. I'm not even talking exclusively about small businesses. As someone who has worked in many global organisations with very high levels of income, I can assure you that sales and profit go up and down. Sometimes, they vary wildly. This is a normal part of business. It is very rare to go up and up and up without some periods of stagnation or even going backwards. And depending on where you are in your business journey, sometimes you have to slow down in order to prepare to go to a new level.

For instance, in my own journey, between 2019 and 2021, my business grew quickly, which was amazing. But I was starting to burn out. I also found that a lot of my processes and systems were falling over with scaling. They were perfectly fine when it was just me and a smaller operation to oversee, but they didn't work quite as well when I had more balls to juggle.

I didn't have sufficient support in my team to help me adjust as I grew, and I wasn't operating at the version of me that was required to step into the next level. My revenue plateaued for a short period, and it's natural to be nervous when something like that happens. But it can also be a reminder that sometimes you need to stop, pause, restrategise and refresh to leap into your next income level.

For service-based businesses, it might mean slowing down on being busy to create a course or to hire new team members. Anyone who has hired will know that when you first onboard someone new, it actually takes more of your time in training them initially than they will add back.

This is a great example of slowing down to speed up. Yes, it'll suck your time and energy for the first few weeks – or even months – but once your new team member is up and running, you'll free up so much of your time to tick high-vibe tasks off your to do list.

Okay, now we have that out of the way, I want to run through some of the most common problems that business owners come across and complain to me about, and how to solve them:

- A product launch failed
- Having a slow month
- Working too many hours/burnout
- Trying to do everything yourself
- Issues hiring staff

A PRODUCT LAUNCH FAILED

Let me share a story with you about my first launch. When my first course launched, I sold 24 spots, which was amazing. That was 24 paying customers, even though I had no landing page, no proven marketing campaign and no real strategy at all. I didn't even have any kind of sales funnel! I sent an email, posted the content on a few Facebook groups, and off I went. Happy days.

For my next launch, I was pumped. I thought, *This is going to be a huge success.* If that's what I achieved on a bare basics launch, just imagine how I'll go if I actually have a landing page, email sequences and Facebook ads.

I'm going to have a $100,000 launch, I told myself with conviction.

I don't really have to spell out what happened next, do I?

For my second launch, I had five people join. Not 55. Not even 25. Just five.

That was a huge wake-up call for me. It's also a great example of how we can take things for granted when they happen too easily. A few pages back, I talked about how it's the challenges, failures and hard times in business that really teach us how to move forward. When you achieve success too easily and you don't learn the lessons along the way, you can be walking towards a dangerous outcome.

Let's say I had launched my second course, and it was a $100,000 launch. As a coach, how would that serve me when I'm working with a client who has experienced a failed launch or an unexpected poor outcome in their business? I can't relate; my journey has only been on the up and up.

That second 'failed' launch almost broke me. I worked so hard on it. I felt like I was an absolute failure and like I had really let down my family because I had said to my husband: "We need to go all-in on this and invest in Facebook ads." And I spent five-figures on a slick copywriter to help me make sure all the course materials were beyond perfect.

When I only had five paying customers sign up, I realised I'd spent more money building the course than I'd earn running it. With that 'failure', I felt like I was taking money away from the family. I cried every night on the couch for a week. It's probably the lowest I've ever felt as a business owner. I even contemplated shutting down my business for the first time ever.

Of course, that's not what I did. I delivered the course, and it was magical. The five people who showed up were brilliant, inspiring women, who went on to become raving fans, sign on for future programs and recommend me to their friends. I ended up using that course as the blueprint for future courses, so the investment in building it has paid for itself over and over again.

Most importantly, when I'm working with my clients and they're going through a tough time or they're not making enough money, I can relate. When I say, "Oh my gosh, I've been there" – I mean it.

The thing is in business, sometimes it doesn't make sense. Sometimes the stats don't add up, or the sales don't come through. Sometimes what 'should' happen doesn't happen but along the way, you learn some valuable lessons.

How to overcome this?

This is a 'get-through-it problem-solving process' that really helps me.

Step 1: Grieve

When something like this happens, I think it's important to allow yourself to grieve. I did. I literally sat and wallowed in my self-pity for a few days. Sitting with your emotions is a really good thing because it enables you to process, learn and work out what specifically is bothering you. Once I'd worked through those emotions, I had the mental space and clarity to come back to: *why am I doing this? Why did I get started with this business in the first place? What does the big picture look like again?* We don't want to stay in this place for too long, of course. In fact, I've found over time that the grieving period gets shorter and shorter for me, as now I recognise that failures are part of business. But I think it's important to allow ourselves to feel the pain, frustration or disappointment rather than gloss over it.

Step 2: Redefine your goal posts

For me, my purpose is all about empowering women by rewiring their money mindset so they can kick massive goals in their own businesses and lives. When I reconnected to this purpose, I realised it didn't matter if I had 5 people or 105 people in my course; I could still serve and make an impact and help them achieve their goals. When you think about a 'failure' or an experience in your business that didn't generate the outcome you'd expected or hoped for, what actually did work towards achieving your goal?

Step 3: Looking for the learning

Looking at the situation objectively is key. When we're in the middle of something, it can be really easy to go into victim mode and feel like everything is too hard and nothing has worked out. Again, going back to my failed launch example, one of my friends actually sat down with me to objectively look at the launch stats. And she said, "Well, actually, you convert really well off your webinar. You have a really high retention rate in your webinar, you just didn't have enough people in there." It's very hard to see things rationally when you're clouded by emotions. Do you have someone you can turn to, like a coach, trusted friend or business ally, who can help you find the lesson in the experience?

HAVING A SLOW MONTH

This is a common fear when you run a business. In fact, I have clients every single month who confess that their biggest fear is having a slow month, which turns into two slow months… and signals the beginning of the end.

The story people tell themselves in this situation is something like this: "It's all over. The business is done. My success to date was a fluke, and now it's all turned bad."

I totally get it. I've been there, with those niggling doubts and fears scratching their way through my thoughts.

I was coaching a client recently and at the beginning of our call, she was absolutely devastated. She had just experienced the slowest two weeks she has ever recorded, and she was gutted. In that two-week period, she'd had no new enquiries, zero sales, no warm leads signed on – it was as dry as a desert.

"Clare, this is hopeless," she sobbed to me. "Why am I even running this business? It's too stressful, I can't take it."

We can go to a really dark place when our mindset drops into this type of thinking. I let her release her emotions, and then I reminded her: it was only two weeks ago that we'd caught up, and her situation had been entirely different. In fact, she had been so busy in our previous call that she was struggling to cope with the level of work she had, the number of clients she had to service and the level of enquiries coming in.

"That was only two weeks ago!" I reminded her. "This is just a tiny blip in your timeline, and it's possibly a great opportunity to catch up on all the work and clients you already have in your pipeline."

She was catastrophising, worrying that this slow period was the start of everything crashing down, which is not an unusual response when you're a business owner. But it's not a response you have to live with.

How to overcome this?

First of all, slow down. I know it feels like this could be the beginning of the end.

Anyone who suffers from imposter syndrome might think, this is it – the penny has dropped. I've been caught out; I'm not who they think I am, and now everyone knows it! You might think that your luck has finally run out and this is it.

That's not what is happening here.

What is happening? Well… you had a slow period! It's not the end of the world. Look at it with fresh eyes by removing the emotions and looking at the facts. One of the reasons why coaching is so effective is because you have someone with a vested interest in you, looking in from the outside; they can often see things that you can't.

Next, work out, what is your action plan? Yes, it's been a slow month. But what have you been doing? Can you get back into energetic alignment with your most successful self? Can you really lean into your mindset practices?

Then from a practical sense, have you followed up all your leads? Are you following your marketing strategy? Can you ramp up your activity? Are there partnerships or opportunities you can use to reach a new audience?

The good news? If you're having a slow month client-wise, you'll have plenty of time to work on your mindset and the strategic activities and marketing you need to get business booming again!

WORKING TOO MANY HOURS AND BURNING OUT

Overworking is a very common issue for small business owners.

You may not like hearing this, but this one is well and truly within your control.

It's so easy to play the victim in this story. I know I do it.

But remember: everything that's in your business was created by you.

Every habit, every schedule, every deadline – all set by you, agreed upon by you or designed by you. You have the ability to go back to clients and say: "That timeline isn't possible, would this work instead?" You have the potential to schedule your day with rests and breaks and downtimes.

But most business owners don't do that. We get so busy and caught up in the grind that we end up working more hours than we ever dreamed we could work in a single week, and, from there, we end up resentful and burnt out.

Take my podcast, for example. It's one of my favourite activities in my business. I usually record a couple of podcasts per week – being a guest on other podcasts too – and I find it to be creatively fulfilling, challenging and inspiring.

If I filled my days with countless podcasts, however, and every single week I was podcasting from 6 am till 8 pm, the shine would wear off. I'd reach a point where I'd say: "I don't care how much money I'm making, I'm not doing this anymore."

When you have a busy period in your business, you can navigate it well enough if you know it's an intentionally busy but brief period. You can do it for a short period of time because you know there's (hopefully) going to be a payoff at the end.

But if you're overworked constantly, then that's not sustainable. Those hours will catch up with you; you'll end up exhausted, resentful, and dipping into unhealthy habits to cope.

Generally, as the saying goes, "If you don't make time for your wellness, you'll be forced to make time for your illness."

Overall, it's a nasty situation and one you don't have to suffer through for a moment longer than necessary.

How to overcome this?

Start by asking yourself: what's the core problem here?
Are you working too many hours because:

- There is a short-term project or issue that requires attention?
- You need to hire more staff?
- You need more support at home or in the business?
- Your business has shifted gear, and you need to revisit the overall structure?
- The business model is just not sustainable anymore?

The aim is to work out whether the problem is short-term, and you're able to suck it up, knowing that the benefits on the other side of things will make up for it, or whether it's long-term, and you need a solution, stat.

When you're working through this, I suggest you get a pen and paper (or sit at your computer and tap away) and word dump with the following prompts:

- What do you love about your work?
- What do you not love and can outsource?
- What needs to be done differently?

TRYING TO DO EVERYTHING YOURSELF

"Business is booming. Which is great, but I can't cope – I'm doing it all myself."

These aren't the exact words that fell out of my client's mouth, but they're not far off.

She was exhausted. Burnt out. And much like the previous point I made around working too many hours, her health was suffering as a result.

Fortunately, there's a really simple and powerful solution to this problem: delegate.

Some people have the financial means to delegate, but they're not in the right mindset to delegate. Some people are more than happy to delegate, but they don't have the financial capacity to take that step just yet.

If you're in the first category, then you could take immediate action. Some people will find delegating difficult, especially if you've been in business for a while and you're used to being the person doing all the 'doing'. Because you've always done it, you likely have a really clear idea of how you want it to be done, along with an expectation or preconception that perhaps no one can do it the way you would. It's only natural that you want to ensure the way someone else completes the job is up to your standards and meets your expectations. But if you're struggling with the idea of delegating, my advice is to start small with something you're more than willing to outsource: two hours of bookkeeping per week, for instance, or a proofreader to run their eye over all your marketing materials.

Keep in mind, you're not going to solve this problem unless you delegate. You'll keep doing it all yourself, working long hours, with no end in sight. A lot of this boils down to not having the right support and not intentionally creating a structure and framework that works for you. And this comes back to – you guessed it! – mindset.

If you fall into the second category, then there's another part of this conversation we need to have around privilege. As I've mentioned earlier in this book, I'm very aware of and grateful for the fact that my business is at the stage that it's at, where I can afford to hire support. I also have a supportive partner who believes in my vision for my business, and I recognise that not everyone has that.

But regardless of the cards you've been dealt, you have to put one foot in front of the other and work it out.

How to overcome this?

Get to the bottom of why you're taking on too much, why you're not letting go and what some potential solutions might be. When you really dig into how and why you've ended up here and you do that investigation and sit with the results, you can work out the ideal way forward.

For example, if you run a small digital marketing agency, you might find that you do sales calls; you send and chase invoices; you do all of your own client management; you run your clients' Facebook advertising campaigns and Google ads; you do your own BAS; you take care of business admin, your own business marketing, your social media posts – you get the gist.

It's no wonder you would feel overwhelmed.
If that's the case:

- What are you doing about your current situation? If you don't make changes, nothing changes.

- What support do you need to bring in? This could be in or out of the business – support for your business, your family or your household (this could be paid or unpaid support).

- Are you saying "no" enough? This could mean saying no to more clients or money – which can be triggering if you have money mindset issues around 'not having enough'. But if you say yes to everyone else all the time, you have to understand there will be a cost.

- What is the cost of not changing? What is the impact on your health (mentally and physically) if you stay in this stressed state indefinitely?

- Who do you need to be to get the outcomes that you want? Ultimately, the only person who can improve your life is you.

HOW TO DELEGATE AND SET YOUR CALENDAR FREE

To add structure and support to your day, these are some tasks you could delegate to free up your time and reduce your overwhelm.

IF YOU'RE IN A POSITION TO INVEST IN HELP, CONSIDER:

- **Hiring a virtual assistant (VA) to manage your inbox.** People make the mistake of thinking they personally need to be in their email all the time, but a good VA can streamline it all for you and only bring the most urgent messages to your attention.

- **Handing over management of your calendar, too.** A VA can schedule appointments, rearrange meetings and make sure your day flows smoothly for you.

- **Outsourcing the parts of your role you don't enjoy.** Creating graphics, uploading videos, scheduling my podcast: these are all aspects of my job that don't set my soul on fire, so I'll happily outsource them to someone else who can get the job done for me and free up my time to do what I love – coaching.

- **Get help outside of your business.** What are your most hated jobs and tasks around the house or in your personal life? There's a good chance you could outsource them. For example, hire a cleaner, get a nanny to do the school run or shuttle kids to after-school activities, book a handyman to take care of home repairs, or pay a gardener to mow the lawns and keep the weeds at bay.

IF YOU'RE NOT IN A POSITION TO INVEST IN HELP, HERE ARE SOME IDEAS:

- **Do service swaps.** As I've mentioned previously, swapping services with another like-minded professional can be a great way of gaining value for your business without a financial outlay. Just make sure it's an even swap, that is, don't exchange $3,000 of your value for $300 of theirs, and you'll both walk away happy.

- **Employ junior cadets or students.** They're still training, so your investment in a part-time student will be far less than a full-time professional. They'll benefit, as they're still learning the theory, and you can engage them to start getting some practical hands-on experience.

- **Do the tasks that drain your energy first.** These are the things you least look forward to each week, fortnight or month, the ones you put off so they always hang on your to do list. If you can knock these over earlier in the morning, you'll feel so motivated to have the task in your rear-view mirror that you'll enjoy a nice bump in dopamine to motivate you forward for the rest of your day!

ISSUES HIRING STAFF

I've saved this one for last because this is the big one.

Hiring staff can be a minefield, for so many different reasons.

There are the money blocks: Can I even afford this person?

The fears around getting it wrong: What if I hire someone and they're a dud?

The concerns around workplace culture: We're so happy right now. What if this person changes the dynamic?

The biggest pain point for most business owners is finding the right fit and then ensuring that they're managing the person they do hire so they're getting the most out of them. The fear of getting this wrong can keep people stuck and prevent them from taking action, which means they don't have the support staff they need to grow and scale the way they want to.

How to overcome this?

I have a proven three-step process for hiring staff, and it's absolutely foolproof. Not because it means you will hire the right person every time – that's definitely not the case! But this process allows the space, time and flexibility to move on quickly if things don't quite turn out.

Here we go:

Step 1: Hire slowly

Don't rush in. Finding the right person is much more important than finding someone fast. Don't hire your brother's girlfriend or your friend's cousin based solely on a recommendation, either – be professional about it. After all, this is your money you're investing into this person.

So, do everything the same way you would if you worked in a big business. Read their CV in detail, interview them (preferably multiple times) and check their references – actually call them, don't just rely on written testimonials. Start with a trial and include a probation period. Schedule regular check-ins so you can both give feedback about how the role is going.

DO ALL OF IT. Don't skip any step. The easiest way to cause issues is to fast-track this process, so don't be tempted to go for the quick solution.

Step 2: Fire quickly

The same way you know when it's not the right match in a romantic relationship, you know when it's not the right fit in a business sense.

If you hire someone and it's not working out, move them on as quickly as possible. Yes, this can be a little tricky if you did go ahead and hire your brother's girlfriend or your friend's cousin and there's an impact outside of work. But that needs to be secondary to your business goals.

If you think there's a way to continue working together with some clear feedback, boundaries and benchmarks, then go for it. But if you don't see a clear path forward, rip the bandaid off sooner rather than later. You've intentionally hired this person to make your life easier so if that's not the reality of the situation, it's time to move them on.

If you're still within the probation period, this is a quick and straightforward process, although the conversations you need to have might cause you some stress. Which leads me to my third step…

Step 3: Have direct conversations

Some people think that being direct is awkward. My experience is the exact opposite – by being more direct, the expectations are clear. A lack of communication leads to misaligned expectations, which then breeds resentment.

Being direct may not come naturally to you, but there are some things you can do to improve the outcome of the conversation:

- **It starts with mindset.** You can give direct feedback and still be a nice person – these are not mutually exclusive. In fact, in my view, it's actually kinder to give people clear feedback and expectations than to pretend everything is fine and fire them out of the blue.

- **Get the timing right.** If you do give feedback on the spot, sometimes it might not be worded in the most eloquent way. It can be beneficial to sleep on it so you can consider the most positive and productive way to word your feedback. On the flip side, don't leave giving feedback so long that the actual moment is now days or weeks in the past and the context is less relevant.

- **Practice makes perfect.** You're not always going to get it right, especially when you're just starting out. You'll figure out what works and what doesn't over time, but don't be afraid of getting it 'wrong'. It can help to model other people that navigate this world. I had a manager I really admired, and I still model his approach when I'm having direct conversations.

In a chapter about problem-solving, it would be remiss of me not to mention the incredible role that resilience plays in all of this. All problems – no matter how big or insurmountable they seem – have a solution. As with many things in life, it's how we adapt our mindset to tackle them that will have the greatest impact on how we move forward.

At the risk of sounding trite, all problems can be solved in some way, shape or form.

There's always a choice involved; sometimes, the consequences of those choices can be very far-reaching. But when you develop your 'resilience muscles' by facing each challenge head-on, recognising the core of the issue, then developing a solution, you begin to understand that anything that doesn't break you truly does make you stronger. Hopefully, you take the loss, learn the lesson, and move on a little more armed and prepared for what comes next.

We all have those days where we think, *Screw it, I don't want to do it anymore!* where we scroll through Seek, romanticising what it would be like to work for someone else. Daydreaming about how much less stressful it would be if we didn't have to steer the ship anymore and no longer had to be responsible for everyone and everything…

There are some downsides to running a business, but there are also so many upsides. Life-changing upsides. It's a game-changer when you realise that your ability to move forward, to conquer your challenges and to succeed is all within you because – at the risk of sounding like a broken record – it all comes back to mindset.

*"If it were easy,
everyone would do it."*

"Remember, diamonds are created under pressure, so hold on – it will be your time to shine soon."

– SOPE AGBELUSI –

CHAPTER 7:
Key Points

- Everyone goes through challenges; it's a normal part of owning a business.

- Businesses move in cycles, and growth and success are not always linear. It's okay for your business to plateau at times or even go backwards. Don't get too hung up on results in any one month, quarter or even year. Keep your eye on the long-term outcomes.

- There are a few common problems that business owners face, and the first step towards moving past them is facing them head on. All problems – no matter how big or insurmountable they seem – have a solution.

Your Money Meeting Agenda

- **Get clear on the problems**
    » Identify the biggest challenges that you are facing right now in your business that are preventing you from taking it to the next level.
    » Put pen to paper (or fingertips to keyboard) so you can list all of the challenges you have identified.

- **Get matchmaking**
    » Start brainstorming solutions to match with each potential or existing problem. What are some options or actions you could take – even if they don't feel like realistic options right now?

- » The point here is to brainstorm anything and everything you can do to address the situation so you can create a clear road map out of it. Write down any and all ideas.
- » Hint: if it feels too hard, pretend you're giving someone else advice about their business or problems. Or engage the help of someone else to give their advice: a coach or a business friend.

- **Break the solutions down into bite-sized next steps**
  - » Even if you can't take the ideal next action, what are the baby steps you could take? For example, if you realise you'd ideally like to hire a marketing manager to drive new growth and unlock new revenue, but financially that's not feasible, can you engage a marketing contractor for five hours per week? Or if you're working too many hours and suffering from burnout and you're dreaming about a week off lying by the beach, can you schedule three hours off every Friday morning to escape to the beach for a walk, a meditate and a refresh?

CHAPTER 8:

INTENTIONAL GRATITUDE, GROWTH AND EXPANSION

Imagine you've stepped off a plane in the Maldives and as you inhale the salty air at your resort, you're feeling fresh and relaxed because you just flew business class. You're checking in with someone you love, and you're escorted to your stunning suite overlooking the water by your own private butler.

Your overwater bungalow looks out into the crystal clear water and as you arrive in your room, you see a bottle of Dom Perignon and crystal glasses. You have your own private swimming pool, and you admire the fish swimming below your feet, under the glass-bottomed floor.

A fresh fruit platter arrives, and your butler advises that the masseuse will arrive for your massage within the hour. This is your annual trip to the Maldives, and, this time, you're excited about the private tours the hotel has arranged for you to islands you haven't yet seen on your many previous visits.

This is not a 'once in a lifetime' experience for you, nor have you chewed through your life savings in order to make this happen.

This is your 'normal'. This is the level of expansion and abundance and wealth you live in every day, and it only gets better from here.

How does this sound to you?

Are you all in? Are you mentally packing your bags and thinking about who you want to take with you on your next visit?

Does this seem like a realistic lifestyle you could achieve in your future?

Or – does this whole concept trigger you? Do you read this story and think I'm describing someone else's life, which could never possibly be yours?

The first step in creating exceptional wealth is recognising something you desire and allowing yourself to believe that it's something that is possible for you.

I used to think that for someone to be really wealthy, they had to be exceptionally smart, beautiful, educated, eloquent, connected, charismatic and more. The list of 'qualifiers' I had in my head around what it required to gain big wealth was huge.

But as I have had the opportunity to get closer to wealth – to experience being around significantly wealthy people – the more I realised that anyone can be wealthy.

Including me! Ordinary me.

And including you.

You can create the most abundant, amazing and fulfilled life – even if it seems way out of reach right now.

In the last few chapters, I've taken you through a number of practical steps, tips and strategies to help you really kick your business into gear and adopt habits and tools to thrive. This is all really exciting, meaningful, powerful stuff.

But now, this is where it all comes together in terms of the end result, or the big, expansive, exciting, life-changing, new 'you'.

So, what is the secret to getting from where you are now to where you want to be?

STOP 'WHEN'-ING YOURSELF

You might have had the thought, *I'll be happier or more successful when [insert thing here] happens.*

As a coach, I hear variations of these all the time.

"I'll be happier when…

- » I'm making six or seven figures a year…
- » I have the right team in place…
- » I am published in Forbes magazine…
- » I sign my ideal client/s…
- » I lose 20 kg and hit my goal weight…
- » I buy the house of my dreams…
- » I meet the love of my life…"

"When that happens, I'll never be unhappy or stressed or worried about money again."

The problem with these when statements? They're not true.

The reality is, if you feel 'lack' at a certain level, you'll feel that at the next level, too.

Making a million dollars isn't going to magically solve all your problems or change your mindset overnight. You can feel stressed out and overwhelmed, whether you're making $10,000, $100,000 or $10 million out of your business.

The source of your eternal happiness is not in securing the client, losing the weight or gaining the wealth. The battle is waged – and won – in your mind far before the actual 'thing' happens.

The good news about this is, it means you don't have to wait for 'it' to happen in order to sink into that expansive feeling of growth, abundance and success.

You can feel really expansive and elated when the dollar values involved are on the smaller end of the scale. I can remember when I was just starting out and I signed my first client for $1,000 per month, for a six-month package. I was overjoyed. I had happy tears; I was jumping up and down. Five years on, and my six-month package sells for much, much more than that. But at the time, I felt like I had truly 'made it'. My business was thriving!

Just recently, someone I follow on Instagram was celebrating a win. Her business had made five figures, and she was screaming about it from the rooftops. She couldn't believe it and shared that she'd dreamt of hitting this milestone from the moment she started her business.

In my line of work, I follow loads of different coaches and mentors who are at different stages of their business journeys, so it's not uncommon to see people celebrating a five-figure month, or a five-figure week – or even a five-figure day.

But this particular person was celebrating the fact that she'd made $10,000 for the year. It was a beautiful reminder that the dollar figure genuinely isn't the driver of joy or abundance or gratitude – it's the mindset you have, regardless of the money involved.

WHAT DOES IT TRULY MEAN TO LIVE INTENTIONALLY?

The answer to this is going to be different for everyone, depending on your own unique values and beliefs. Living your best, most intentional and profitable life means working out what matters to you on every level – from the very deep and spiritual (this is what I want my legacy to be on this planet) to the somewhat superficial (I want to drive a Ferrari and shop at Louis Vuitton).

I've mentioned many times how I have embraced the practice of living in an expansive mindset, which means I live in the energy of my goals on a day-to-day basis. A really practical example of this is my house. As I mentioned at the start of the book, in 2022, my husband and I bought our beach shack in our dream suburb on our dream street. Now, if you were to come and visit me, you'll see why we call it the beach shack – it's not a big house, and it's certainly not modern or fancy.

And even though we're working towards manifesting that – the big waterfront mansion with a pool and spa, a chef's kitchen and a bedroom-sized walk-in robe – right now, we absolutely adore waking up every day in this home.

Every morning when I make breakfast and look out at the water from my kitchen bench, I pinch myself that this is where we live. I'm excited about what the future holds, while also being super grateful and appreciative of where we are right now.

Even in our last house when we were renting and we didn't live on the water and our lifestyle was different to what it is today, we still lived in that same expansive energy. This is what it means to live intentionally.

A REMINDER TO DREAM BIG

As I've outlined in an earlier chapter, intentional planning is so much fun because it's really about working out what a big, beautiful, abundant life really means to you.

Is it a private yacht?
Is it private planes or flying first class?
Is it having a chef?
Is it having a big chunk of savings in the bank?
Is it investing in a hefty property or share portfolio?
Is it designer handbags and dresses and jewellery?
Is it a cleaner who comes twice a week?
Is it having the financial security to support other family members?
Is it eating out at fancy restaurants every weekend?
Is it supporting charities you care about?
Is it travelling overseas multiple times per year?
Is it owning a holiday home in the snow or at the beach?

I've noticed that people sometimes don't allow themselves to desire things, for myriad reasons.

For instance, you might have a preconceived negative idea of what 'wealthy' people are like. Or maybe you don't think it's possible for you. Or, are you simply not allowing yourself to want that outcome because you don't think it's possible, or achievable, or you're not worth it? The more you pull at these threads, the more clarity you gain about what truly lights you up.

And while I definitely agree that the more money you make, the more choices you have, the real secret to living an amazing, abundant, wealthy, happy life is loving your life now, regardless of how much money is actually sitting in your bank account.

I imagine that you're reading along right now, and at least some of you are thinking, *Oh, that's easy for you to say – you've got plenty of money.*

I totally get it. But I want to illustrate my point by sharing that some of the happiest, richest and most abundant and expansive experiences of my life actually relate to times when I was more or less flat broke.

When I was travelling in Vietnam, I was backpacking and living off a budget. I looked up the next part of my journey, and the bus ride I was about to take was a 24-hour journey, at a price of $6.

There was the option of flying – but it was more expensive. Much more expensive. Like, more than 12 times the cost of a bus fare, at a time when I was carefully planning out how to intentionally spend every single dollar.

After much umming and ahhing, I made the decision to fly. The fare was $79 (I still remember, decades later!). It felt like such a decadent treat, and I remember the elation I felt when I checked in for my flight and sat in my seat, marvelling at the fact that I'd just nixed a 24-hour journey by road and replaced it with a 60-minute flight.

I was travelling on my own at the time, but I'd connected with a couple of people along the way. They took the bus to the next destination. When they noticed I wasn't on the bus, they wondered if I'd missed it. And when they saw me at the other end and I confessed I'd splurged on the plane ticket and flown, their response was incredulous – as if I was a total baller, Miss Moneybags, overflowing with riches.

The feeling of abundance, luxury and 'wealth' I felt in that moment was intoxicating. I remember thinking: I've made it in life!

That feeling is possible whether your lifestyle allows you to 'upgrade' on an $80 flight, an $8,000 business class upgrade or an $80,000 private jet journey. As I've said – and will continue to say! – it's never about the money. It's always about the mindset.

Someone who has the best mindset is my aunty, who lives in Central West Queensland. She lives in an actual shipping container. It's covered in red dirt from the country, and she doesn't have air conditioning, so it's a sweat box during the warmer months.

She owns a lot of land. She used to live in a beautiful house with big wraparound balconies looking out over rolling hills, and when she decided she wanted to go to Central Queensland, she certainly could have bought another beautiful big home.

"But why would I want to?" she says. "I've got everything I want right here. I'm happy. The animals are happy. We've got water in the dam. We're happy with what we have."

My aunty has intentionally created a simple life that, on the outside, may not be full of the trappings of traditional 'wealth'.

But her idea of success and abundance is not another nice house she has to maintain. It's a simple, relaxed life where she has plenty of free time to dedicate to her animals and her gardens.

I'm sharing her story as a reminder that, yes, we want to dream big and reach for the stars and accomplish every crazy goal we set for ourselves. But it's just as important to connect to the feelings that you are wanting to create with the material outcomes, no matter where you are in the journey.

Money can't buy you love… but what does it buy?

Money can't make you happy.

But money does buy you more experiences and more opportunities and more choices.

It's important to be clear on the fact that money in and of itself is not the end goal; it's what it creates that can bring us joy. And in whatever circumstances you find yourself in today, you have that opportunity to create joy.

THE PRACTICE OF GRATITUDE

Gratitude is an incredibly powerful practice you can use to live your best, most intentional life today, while aiming for even more brilliance and greatness in your future.

I call it a practice because that's what gratitude is. I remember when I was first learning about gratitude, and it felt very simplistic and, honestly, not all that helpful.

I had the impression that the people who were talking about being grateful and embracing gratitude were like that because they'd already achieved their goals.

It's easy for you to be grateful because you're already at the happy part! I'd think. You're rich and beautiful and powerful and living your best life.

There were many stories I'd tell myself, and they all amounted to: I can't feel that yet because my business is only in the early stages. Or I can't even afford to buy a house yet. Or I haven't lost my baby weight yet.

What I've discovered over time is that gratitude is not about the specific logistics of your life. It's about (surprise!) the mindset you have in your daily life and the approach you take every single day.

Just start small.

When I began my journey, I began noticing and appreciating small moments in my day. Pausing for an extra moment and cuddling my son, being so grateful that he is alive. Appreciating the deliciousness of a meal I was eating.

From there, it snowballed! I now practice gratitude as a reflex; it's ingrained in my daily way of life. As I've mentioned already, at the time of writing this book, I'm living in a house in my dream location. But the reality is, I'm living in a tiny three-bedroom house, sharing the small third bedroom as an office with my husband every day who also works from home.

This is not my dream house. But we have a big vision for our house, and waking up here every day is a reminder of what we've achieved and what we're working towards. I'm not exaggerating when I say my husband and I wake up every day and we pinch ourselves; we're that blown away with how grateful we are to live here.

If you adopt an attitude of gratitude, you'll learn that the more you do it, the easier it gets.

You'll also discover that you can be grateful for what you have and still desire more. The more that you practice gratitude, the more opportunities open up for you, and you start to invite more into your life.

You can have a healthy and happy child and still really desire to have a second child.

You can have a loving partner and still desire more affection and connection with them.

You can be thrilled you're making five figures per month and still have a goal of earning six figures.

You can be incredibly happy where you live and still dream about your next, nicer house.

This is my vision. But what's yours?

What do you want to create?

What are your big picture, 'pie in the sky' goals for the most abundant, expansive future you can imagine?

RECOGNISING THE MILESTONES

I was talking to a friend recently about how much our generation has changed when it comes to travel. We travel so regularly compared to what it was like when I was growing up.

During my childhood, we didn't travel overseas. In fact, we didn't even travel domestically. As a family of seven (two adults and five children), packing up, getting on a plane and staying in a hotel was an expensive undertaking that was well beyond our financial reach. For us, a holiday was bundling up in the car and driving interstate to a relative's house and crashing on their lounge room floor.

I didn't go overseas until I was 23. First world problem, I know, but to me, it was mind-blowing to recognise just how differently my kids are growing up. My eldest child had been to six different countries before he even started school!

"Times have changed," I told my friend.

"Only 'rich' people travelled a lot when we were kids," I said.

"But these days, most people travel with their families all the time!"

My friend kind of laughed. Then, in a very well-intentioned and kind way, she gave me a big, fat reality check.

"No, Clare, everyone doesn't go overseas," she said. "You just spend more time with people who do."

She was right. The world hasn't fundamentally changed – my place and my viewpoint within it has. It's not that 'more people are travelling', necessarily; it's that more people I know are travelling.

It's an entitled view for me to correlate my experience with the 'normal' experience, and her feedback prompted me to dig a little deeper. The stats show that something like 40 percent of Australians have never left the country[3]. That doesn't marry up with my belief that 'everyone travels overseas nowadays!'

The truth of the matter is: I now live in a different income bracket and am in different social circles to the ones I grew up in. There's absolutely nothing wrong with that. In fact, it's worth celebrating – I've worked really hard and manifested this beautiful, abundant life!

But I also know that it is really beneficial to recognise when you've reached a new milestone in your life. As you level up in your life and your business, you'll start to notice these types of abundant experiences, or as I like to call them: energetic alignments.

The more that you lean into and recognise the things that bring genuine joy and value to your life, the more you'll work out how to prioritise and work towards embracing more of the same.

And, they'll start to show up for you more and more.

So now: it's over to you!

I've given you all the tools and techniques and strategies you need. These are the steps and actions that I have personally used to build my own big, bountiful life, and they're also the same ones I use when mentoring my clients to help them achieve things like…

Smashing new sales targets to make $10k, $50k or even six figures each month.

Manifesting massive goals, wins and collaborations they've wanted for years.

Setting and achieving milestones they could only dream of in the past.

And working to live, rather than living to work.

Remember that achieving big, bold goals and ticking off audacious milestones that seemed unimaginable only a short while ago all start by taking the smallest of baby steps. Earlier, I encouraged you to identify some baby steps you could take in your business that could help you move towards your most intentional, most profitable life. If you haven't already, I want you to start taking action on these as soon as possible. As soon as you start putting that energy out there, the sooner you'll start to see results.

After all, a savings account starts with putting $1 in it. The more you delay putting that $1 aside, the longer you'll wait for your life to change. Life is far too short to sit around waiting on the sidelines for things to happen for you when you can make them happen all on your own!

So, take this as your call to arms to get started on making positive changes now.

Your business is your engine that can empower you to start creating your life. With the insights and strategies in this book, you know how to get out there and achieve everything you want. We've spoken about how to create more profit and how to translate that into the business and the life you want to create.

Now, it's all yours for the taking. It's time to step up and do it!

CHAPTER 8

Key Points

- You don't have to be super smart, beautiful, educated, powerful, connected, famous or anyone 'special' in order to be wealthy beyond your wildest dreams. No-one has more 'right' to be wealthier than anyone else.

- No matter who you are or what your current circumstances are, if you have the right tools in front of you, you can create wealth.

- You'll never be happier 'when' something happens or changes. And it's much more fun to shift your mindset and sink into the expansive energy of joy and growth now, rather than waiting for 'it' to happen and make you happy (whatever 'it' is).

Living intentionally is truly about dreaming big and then taking actions – some small, some big – to move you from where you are today to where you ultimately want to be. You can live your dream life – I'm proof of that!

Your Money Meeting Agenda

- **Identify your biggest dreams and desires**
    - » As you settle into the expansive energy of creating your dream business, working with your dream clients, earning your dream income and living your dream life, spend an hour journaling what this life really looks like for you.

Get really specific! Consider things like…
- » Where do you live? In what type of house?
- » What is your daily routine like?
- » What are your hobbies?
- » Who do you spend time with?
- » What are your travel routines?
- » What causes or charities do you want to contribute to?
- » What excites you?

- **Write to 'present you' from 'future you'**
  - » Write in the present tense, as if you've actually achieved all of these goals and you're already living this life. Expand on how you are feeling in the future, and the steps you took to get there. Share any advice that 'future you' has for 'present you'.

- **Stay accountable**
  - » It's all well and good to be fired up about creating your most profitable business and next-level life but unless you actually take action, you won't move forward.
  - » Set yourself regular money meetings to focus on your business profit and revisit your goals.
  - » Find yourself a coach, high-level community or mastermind to keep you inspired and on track to your deepest desires.

WHAT NEXT?

Now that you understand the energetics of money mindset and also the practical foundations of profit…

Now that you have a firm grip on the power of intentional investing, in terms of its ability to drive massive leaps in growth and profitability…

Now that you're clear not just on the steps you need to take, but also the person you need to become in order to step into your best, most dynamic, most profitable and most successful self…

And now that you know you have just as much right and opportunity to create an incredible, abundant future as anyone else…

Now that you know ALL of this, I hope this is just the start of your journey into making more money, enjoying more profit and creating the most abundant, beautiful life you can imagine.

You are worthy and deserving of everything you desire.

Master your Money.

Master your Mindset.

Maximise your Growth.

"If you always do what you've always done, you'll always get what you've always got."

— HENRY FORD —

ACKNOWLEDGEMENTS

First and foremost, I want to thank Sarah Megginson, my ghostwriter, who helped me put this book together in a cohesive and meaningful way. Not only are you an incredibly talented writer but also a beautiful human and now a dear friend. I am beyond grateful to have undertaken this journey with you.

Next I want to thank the love of my life, my husband, Shannon. Writing a book has been a big undertaking of time and investment of money, and he has been incredibly supportive and has believed in me every step of the way. Shannon — I absolutely adore you, and my life simply would not be as incredible as it is without you in it.

Thank you to my awesome kids, who have been hearing about 'Mum's book' for years and supporting me with lots of cuddles.

I want to thank my family: my mum, Denise, my dad, Ian, and my siblings, Julie, Andrew, Trent and Kara. We didn't have a lot of money growing up, but we had a ton of love and laughs, and we still do to this day. I am so proud of how everyone in our family has worked hard to create amazing lives for themselves. Thank you also to Toni and Chrissy for all your support.

A shoutout to my biz besties: Anna, Brooke, Emily, Steph, Anita and Bec. This business game ain't easy, and I am so grateful for your support over the years.

My mentors and coaches over the years: in particular, Denise Duffield-Thomas, Ruby Lee, Suzy Ashworth and Brigit Esselmont. You've inspired me, lifted me up, and witnessed the tears and the elation at various phases of my journey, and I will be forever grateful to you.

To my team. Sally, you have been my right-hand person in business, and your patience, talent and reliability are second to none. I am eternally grateful to you, and I appreciate you so much. To Dan, Leah, Drie, Kirsty and Anna, I appreciate you so much, and you have all played such a pivotal role in my business journey to date.

A big thank you to Dean Publishing for believing in me and this book and for bringing it to life – and to all the partners and media who help get more eyeballs on this book.

Thank you to my clients and students from over the years. I know that self-development work isn't easy, and I honour you for pushing through this discomfort to implement changes to create a better business and life. I have loved teaching you about money and witnessing the incredible transformations that you have undertaken.

And last but not least, I want to thank you, the reader. Thank you for choosing this book. I am so excited that you have decided to focus on money and creating changes in your life. I trust you will take the learnings from this book and implement them to uplevel your mindset and live your most amazing and intentional life.

ABOUT THE AUTHOR

Clare Wood is a money mentor, writer, speaker and podcaster. She is also a gym junkie, drinker of wine, passionate traveller, wrangler of two young boys, manifestor, numbers nerd and reality TV addict, who lives in her waterfront home by the beach.

Clare is a qualified accountant (CPA), but she's not your average bean counter. As founder of The Profit Academy, she uses her money-making, mentoring powers for good, helping people scale their service-based businesses, while creating lifestyles they love.

Clare uses proven and practical money management principles combined with powerful mindset work to support her clients to make more money. She believes everyone has money stories that limit their ability to earn more. When you transform your relationship with money, you can rapidly increase the amount of profit you earn and create a life of financial freedom and fun.

clarewood.com

ENDNOTES

1 Kollewe, J 2018, 'Twitter makes first quarterly profit in its history', *The Guardian*, viewed 2 December 2022, https://www.theguardian.com/technology/2018/feb/08/twitter-makes-first-quarterly-profit-history

2 Pape, S 2017, *The Barefoot Investor*, John Wiley & Sons, Milton, Queensland, Australia, p 54.

3 Scott, K 2019, 'Why many Australians don't have overseas travel on their bucket list', *ABC Everyday*, viewed 2 December 2022, https://amp.abc.net.au/article/everyday/10725770.

NOTES

www.ingramcontent.com/pod-product-compliance
Lightning Source LLC
Chambersburg PA
CBHW050417120526
44590CB00015B/1999